W0009446

A Year *with* Father Rutler

GEORGE WILLIAM RUTLER

A YEAR

with

FATHER RUTLER

Lent, Easter,
and Spring

VOLUME 2

EDITED BY DUNCAN MAXWELL ANDERSON

SOPHIA INSTITUTE PRESS

Manchester, New Hampshire

Sophia Institute Press
Box 5284, Manchester, NH 03108
1-800-888-9344

www.SophiaInstitute.com

Sophia Institute Press® is a registered trademark of Sophia Institute.

2017 edition
Library of Congress Cataloging-in-Publication Data

Names: Rutler, George W. (George William), author.
Title: A year with Father Rutler : a pastor speaks to his people / George
    William Rutler ; edited by Duncan Maxwell Anderson.
Description: Manchester, New Hampshire : Sophia Institute Press, 2017. |
    Includes bibliographical references.
Identifiers: LCCN 2017024886 | ISBN 9781622823840 (leatherbound : alk. paper)
Subjects: LCSH: Church year meditations. | History, Modern—21st
    century—Miscellanea.
Classification: LCC BX2170.C55 R884 2017 | DDC 242/.3—dc23 LC record available at https://lccn.loc.gov/2017024886

2019 edition
978-1-64413-266-1 (vol. 1)
978-1-64413-269-2 (vol. 2)
978-1-64413-272-2 (vol. 3)
978-1-64413-275-3 (vol. 4)
978-1-64413-278-4 (4-volume set)

Library of Congress Control Number:2019954891

First printing

The publication of *A Year with Father Rutler*
was made possible through the generosity of:

Sean Fieler
Joseph J. Frank
William Grace
Mr. and Mrs. Vincenzo La Ruffa
Mr. And Mrs. Arthur S. Long

CONTENTS

Lent

Taking the Plunge 3

I Have Seen God in a Man 5

Ears to Hear 7

Faith, Not Sentiment 9

"The Acquisition of the Last End" 11

Good versus Evil 13

The Cross Is Not a Misfortune 15

The Turkish Bell Tolls 17

Satan's Enemy 19

"You Will Strengthen Your Brethren" 21

Walking Is Better Than Flying 23

The Temptations of the Church 25

What Is "Genius"? 27

The Seven "Helps" 29

You Are There 31

Knowing and Unknowing 33

Smartphones and Sociopaths 35

The Battles of Body and Soul 37

The Trance of God 39

Like Light Appearing 41

With Him on the Holy Mountain 43

"Have I Been So Long with You, Philip?" 45

Pirates 47

Laetare, Ierusalem 49

The Hatred Whose Name We Dare Not Speak (Genocide) 51

Salvation or Narcissism 53

Evidence of Birth 55

Making the Best of Our days 57

A Benevolent Plan for Each Soul 59

"He Who Believes Shall Be Saved" 61

The Courage to Continue 63

The Secret of Joy 65

House of Grace 67

Humility Simplifies 69

Your Step Gets Firm and Sure 71

The Sanhedrin Today 73

Allegory 75

The Gate of Mercy 77

Faithful Thomas 79

Salvation from the Ultimate Slavery 81

The One Drama That Is Real 83

Greatness and Goodness 85

A Loftier Judgment 87

Christ Enters the City 89

The Flesh and Blood of This Jesus 91

Eastertide

You, O Death, Are Annihilated 95

Christ Is Risen! 99

The Sublime Wayfarer 101

Transformation 103

Meet Him in the Blessed Sacrament 105

Joy Is a Fact 107

"Gold and Silver Have I None" 109

The Work Ahead of Us 111

Beyond All Deserving 113

Joy That Is Not of This World 115

A Mystery Old and New 117

To Proclaim the Resurrection 119

Eternal Beauty 121

Thomas Had No Doubt 123

"An Eye for the Times" 125

Living with His Life Instead of Our Own 127

Generosity and the Lord's Mercy 129

The Devil Sends His Compliments 131

To Obey God Instead of Men 133

No Small Details 135

Acting Catholic 137

A Spiritual Engine 139

The Name 141

Wolves and the Shepherd 143

The Soul at Ease 145

Total Change — and Its Efficient Cause 147

The Ascension of Our Lord

Now Has the Son of Man Been Glorified 149

A Great Prince, a Greater Saint 151

Ordinary Magnificence 153

Holiness, Not Entertainment 155

Visible and Invisible 157

Obvious Truth 159

"It Is the Lord!" 161

Good Memories 163

Crowning Glory 165

Protection from Error 167

The Lights of Divinity 169

Civility and Evil 171

Heaven's First Law 173

The Holy Spirit 175

Published Ignorance 177

You Shall Be My Witnesses 179

Always a Gift 181

Yes, Our Bodies Are Sacred 183

Strategist of the Soul 185

Joy and Holy Fear 187

Patience 189

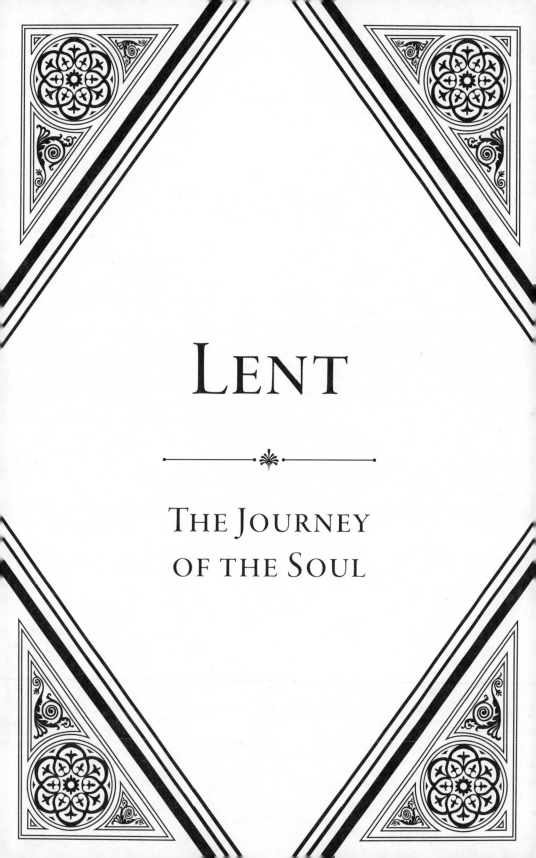

LENT

❧

THE JOURNEY
OF THE SOUL

TAKING THE PLUNGE

Duc in altum. Cast into the deep — or, take the plunge. Christ said it to His disciples (Luke 5:4). When they did as they were told, they caught an astonishing number of fish, and then they left everything and followed him (Luke 5:11). When Bishop Hippolytus of Caesarea wrote down the oral traditions of the lives of the Twelve, he was about as close to the Resurrection as we are to the birth of Antonio Salieri and the death of Johann Sebastian Bach, whose music still lives with us.

Andrew preached in Bulgaria and was crucified on an olive tree in Greece. Bartholomew preached in India and was crucified with his head downward in the part of Armenia that now is in the former Soviet state of Georgia. James, son of Alphaeus was stoned to death in Jerusalem, and James, son of Zebedee, was beheaded by the tetrarch Herod. His brother John, the only apostle known not to have died violently, was exiled to the island of Patmos by the emperor Domitian, later going to Turkey and dying in Ephesus during the reign of Trajan. Matthew died in Hieres near present-day Tehran.

Peter shared his remembrances with Mark and was crucified in Rome. After preaching in Pontus, Galatia, Cappadocia, Betania, Italy, and Asia, Philip was crucified with his head downward in Hierapolis in eastern Turkey during the reign of Domitian. Simon the Zealot was the second bishop of Jerusalem but is said to have also preached in Egypt and Persia, where he was sawed to pieces. Thaddeus, who preached in Edessa and throughout Mesopotamia, was axed to death in Syria. Thomas preached throughout Persia and was speared to death at Calamene in India. Only Judas killed himself, never having left Jerusalem.

The point is that these men did not live superficial lives. They took the plunge and fulfilled the promise of the Master that they would become fishers of men. They did not leave their homes and families and their businesses just to follow a theory, for, as Newman said, "No man will be a martyr for a conclusion."[1] They willingly died in the glory of the Resurrection, which they had seen.

Socrates, having said that the unexamined life is not worth living, changed the lives of many, who passed on what they had learned. None of his disciples, however, and no disciple of any other teacher, could say with St. Paul, who was chosen after the Master had risen from the dead: "It is no longer I who live but Christ who lives in me" (Gal. 2:20). Plato never said that Socrates lived in him; but if Socrates had lived long enough to take the plunge with the untutored fishermen, he might have found a good Greek term for the indwelling of Christ, the sanctifying grace, that moves men to leave everything and die telling others what happened to them.

February 14, 2016

---

[1] John Henry Newman, "An Essay in Aid of a Grammar of Assent," no. 3.

I Have Seen God in a Man

L ent is a time we put away the old man and put on the new. Certain "corporal mortifications," which strengthen us by self-discipline, such as confession and different forms of fasting, are part of this, but more important are increased acts of charity, such as almsgiving. The end of all this is to unwrap the self and to grow into the stature of Christ: "If I give all I possess to the poor and surrender my body to the flames, but have not love, I gain nothing" (1 Cor. 13:3).

It was a special blessing for me last week to conduct a retreat in France at the shrine of St. John-Marie Vianney in Ars and in the nearby ancient cathedral of Lyons. Some thirty priests from New York attended along with our archbishop, Timothy Dolan, who offered Mass each day, and we received the Precious Blood from Vianney's own chalice. Although the Curé d'Ars personally lived a life of total selflessness and acute mortifications, he bought the finest sacred vessels and vestments for God's glory. Our culture tends to make the self rich and God poor, and of course, that never works. The original church of Ars was a very humble structure, so tiny that it held only a handful of people, and when Vianney arrived there in 1817, he found it crumbling from neglect following the French Revolution. But he was confident that God would do great things there, and it happened—all because Vianney was a prodigy of humility, willing to unwrap himself and cloak his people with charity. When one skeptic met him, all he could say was, "I have seen God in a man." He had encountered the sanctifying grace that Christ wills for all of us: "I have been crucified with Christ, and it is no longer I who live but Christ who lives in me" (Gal. 2:20).

Lent is such a brief time that it seems to end almost as soon as it begins, but such also is life itself, and the purpose of Lent is to make precisely that point. The ashes yield quickly to Alleluias for those who outgrow themselves.

February 21, 2010

EARS TO HEAR

Three times the Evangelists preserved Our Lord's words from the original Aramaic:

- when He cried out from the Cross, "My God, my God, why has thou forsaken me?" (Matt. 27:46)
- when He raised from the dead the daughter of Jairus (Mark 5:41)
- when He healed the man who had been deaf from birth (Mark 7:34)

That *Ephphatha*—"Be opened"—in the last instance, was a sign that Our Lord opens human consciousness to a full awareness of God. The Latin word for deaf—*surdus*—gives us "absurd," and the ultimate absurdity is to deny the existence of God and His appeal to the human soul.

I recently had the privilege of preaching at the funeral in Memphis, Tennessee, of a most devout Catholic, Dr. John Shea, who invented the basic surgery on the inner ear that enabled him personally to cure more than forty thousand deaf people, and that has cured probably millions around the world. Years ago, he was most insistent that I not eulogize him, but rather preach the Resurrection. That was easy to do, for his own life was summed up in the words of another John, the Beloved Apostle, who exulted in the Risen Lord: "That which was from the beginning, what our ears have heard ..." (1 John 1:1).

Dr. Shea would often tell patients born deaf that he could let them hear, but that leaving behind the silent world in which they had lived, in many ways beautiful without the noise of life, could be a shock. Many opted to remain deaf. For them it was a prudent choice, for they could hear God better in the way they had known: "Be still and know that I am God" (Ps. 46:10).

Unlike physical deafness, moral deafness is a tragedy more than a disability. Selfish pride hardens the heart so that it hears but does not listen. There are examples of that in the public sphere, as many choose to be willfully ignorant while atrocities are committed. The vile anti-Semitism in Europe of recent years is chillingly reminiscent of the 1930s when so many covered their ears to the lamentations from the ghettos and concentration camps. The slaughter of twenty-one Coptic Christians in Libya was the latest outrage after countless beheadings, crucifixions, or forced exiles of Christians from their ancient homelands, and the destruction of more than one thousand churches in Nigeria. All this has fallen on the morally deaf ears of those who will not acknowledge palpable evil.

During each of these Lenten days, Christ says, "Be opened." Every Christian is commissioned by the Holy Spirit to pass that voice on to others who are tempted to live in moral silence. When Jesus preached His parable of the Sower, He described how His voice sometimes is ignored, or heard only superficially, or rejected in tough times. But those who absorb that sound from Heaven accomplish great things many times over. Having said that, He shouted: "Those who have ears to hear, let them hear!" (see Matt. 11:15).

February 22, 2015

FAITH, NOT SENTIMENT

We can do good things without God, but they do not add up to much in the end. Jesus says that no one is good save his Father (Mark 10:18), but He also bids us to be perfect (Matthew 5:48). This is not contradictory: no amount of human excellence can match God, but God's goodness can enter the human soul, and this is perfection.

Outward acts such as fasting, abstinence, almsgiving, and prayer make the soul available to God's grace; but if these acts are not inspired by faith in God, they become substitutes for God. Jesus exposed that kind of ritual formalism: "Not everyone who says to me, 'Lord, Lord' will enter the kingdom of heaven, but only the one who does the will of my Father in heaven" (Matt. 7:21). Attempts at being good without God's perfecting grace turn religion into sentimentality. In the nineteenth century, Matthew Arnold said that religion is "morality touched by emotion."[2] In that kind of vagueness, morality soon goes out the window, and only emotion is left.

Consider the Beatles' emotive song "All You Need Is Love." It is evidence that in pop culture, any kind of doggerel can sound profound if it is amplified loudly enough by singers with pained faces. The first verse is: "Love, love, love, love, love, love, love, love, love." After those nine incantations of "love," the second verse tells us, "There's nothing you can do that can't be done." I defy anyone to explain that. It is meaningless; but that is what you get when love dissolves into sentiment. To the contrary, "God is spirit, and his worshippers must worship in spirit and

---

[2] Matthew Arnold, *Literature and Dogma* 1, 2.

in truth" (John 4:24). When spirit and truth combine, you get more than mere emotional nonsense: "If I speak in the tongues of men and of angels, but have not love, I am a noisy gong or a clanging cymbal" (1 Cor. 13:1). St. Catherine of Siena explained perfection by saying "The soul cannot live without love, but always wants to love something, because she is made of love, and, by love, I created her."[3] Love must be an active offering of the self to the truth of God.

The way of perfection is the way of truth—not a sensual alternative to truth. The history of false religions is a catalogue of how they confuse truth with emotion and then fall into decay when sentimentality no longer sustains them. When Mary Queen of Scots was beheaded in 1587, witnesses were unsettled to see her lips keep moving for some minutes. Religion that is "morality touched by emotion" is like that. It becomes a quivering appendage, cut off from its vital source. Our Lord saw that in the shadow of the Temple: "These people honor me with their lips, but their hearts are far from me" (Matt. 15:8). And then there was the Judas kiss.

March 13, 2011

---

[3] See *Dialogues* 51.

"THE ACQUISITION OF THE LAST END"

In Lent the Liturgy calls these forty days a joyful season. Without a right understanding of the meaning of true happiness, this can seem forced, a self-conscious "grin and bear it" cheerfulness. Our cultural environment supposes that happiness is essentially a subjective feeling. "Follow your own bliss," wrote a popular writer on religious myth. But Jesus warned us in many ways that although we can follow our own bliss all the way to Heaven, we can follow it all the way to Hell, too.

Feeling happy is not happiness. So G.K. Chesterton (try one of his books for Lenten reading) said that a pessimist is an unhappy idiot, and an optimist is a happy idiot. Idiocy is the limitation of reference to the self. The self-absorbed cannot attain true happiness, for such happiness is an objective involvement with truth outside the self, and ultimately with God. Only the ignorant think that ignorance is bliss. Were that really true, our culture would be Bliss Itself. St. Thomas Aquinas calls happiness "the acquisition of the last end."[4] Happiness is achieving what we were made for. For the man who thinks that life is only an accident of chromosomes, happiness will be nothing more than a whim. But, in fact, God made us to serve Him on earth so that we might delight in Him forever in Heaven.

Sources of temporary happiness, such as wealth and fame and pleasure, become destructive if they are indulged for their own sakes. Only when wealth is used to promote goodness, and fame reflects goodness, and pleasure is taken in goodness, can they lead to happiness. Even then,

---

[4] Thomas Aquinas, *Summa Theologica*, I-II, Q. 1, art. 8.

they can only lead to it. The greatest happiness is the Beatific Vision, seeing forever the uncreated goodness and truth of God.

Many have ridiculed the nineteenth-century professor of logic Richard Whately, who said, "Happiness is no laughing matter." I think he has had the last laugh. The happiness of which he spoke is beyond the capacity of jocularity, although the outward smile is a serene tribute to it. St. Teresa of Avila prayed to be spared from gloomy saints. God came to us in Christ to show us our purpose, and to lead us to it. "Take up your cross" is not a pathology of suffering for its own sake, but a movement of the self beyond the self, to reach our ultimate purpose with God, a happiness that has no end.

February 17, 2002

GOOD VERSUS EVIL

The forty days of Lent are an approximate "tithe" of the days of the year. Spending roughly one-tenth of the year taking stock of our souls and the health of our culture is a wise investment. The sage says that the unexamined life is not worth living. A proper examination, however, needs a good standard of reference. One can hardly examine the human condition properly without reference to good and evil.

Our culture lapsed into a kind of moral delinquency for many years. By that, I mean the social outlook and personal consciousness had grown fuzzy about what goodness and evil mean. A therapeutic attitude replaced moral belief, so that "feeling well" became the equivalent of goodness, and people began to think that nothing is intrinsically evil, with the result that perpetrators of evil were considered victims of circumstance and environment. "Be well" replaced "Good-bye" (which means "God be with you"). And "sharing feelings" came to be the equivalent of witnessing to the truth. Indeed, many people came to think that there is no objective truth. The Pope addressed this philosophical sickness in the encyclicals *Fides et Ratio* and *Veritatis Splendor*.

Truth is truth, whether acknowledged or not. In a conversation with a theologian, a professor who was a lapsed Catholic said that belief in any moral absolutes was a medieval conceit. He challenged the theologian to name one persuasive moral absolute. The theologian replied: "Thou shalt not kill a professor."

I spoke at a luncheon last week, after introductory remarks by Congressman Dick Armey. What he said was very much like a homily. He had come to realize how much good and evil a government can do. He did not say a government can be helpful or corrupt. He spoke deliberately of good and evil. President Reagan once spoke of an "evil empire," and President Bush has spoken of an "axis of evil." Both shocked some commentators who still prefer therapeutic language instead of the stark realities of a fallen world. September 11 made it increasingly difficult to ignore these deep facts of life and death.

Lent begins with a description of Our Lord confronting Satan in the wilderness. Christ endured the temptations to materialism, power, and unreality. He did this on our behalf, for only He can perfectly overcome those expressions of evil. God allows us to be tempted in order to purify our virtue, and so that we may console one another. We are never tempted beyond the power of His grace to overcome evil with good. This is the great message of Lent.

February 24, 2002

THE CROSS IS NOT A MISFORTUNE

In a recent Sunday Angelus address, Pope Benedict said that Lent is "a time of particular commitment in the spiritual combat that places us against the evil present in the world, in each one of us and around us.... A resolution resonating especially urgently for us Christians is the call of Jesus to each take up our own 'cross' and follow him with humility and trust (cf. Matt. 16:24)."

Over the years, the Pope has stressed attention to the Cross, rather than ourselves, in the Eucharistic Liturgy. The novelty of the priest facing the people from the far side of the altar during the Eucharistic Prayer has a tendency to create a self-referential circle of congregation and celebrant closed in upon itself rather than allowing priest and people together to turn toward the Lord. While the newer posture was implemented after the Second Vatican Council, it was not indicated by the council itself and was based on misinformation about early Christian practice. The Pope has been concerned that the radical innovation of the priest not facing eastward with the people may give the impression of the Mass as a solipsistic and horizontal dialogue between priest and people, celebrating the congregation rather than Christ, instead of a vertical offering to the Father of His Son Crucified and Resurrected.

The ideal, preserved in venerable universal tradition, would be the restoration of the priest leading the people on the same side of the altar as together they face liturgical East, the place from which the Glory of the Lord shines upon the Church. We already do that in occasional celebrations of the Extraordinary use of Blessed John XXIII, but it can be adapted to the Novus Ordo use as well, and the Pope is encouraging a gradual recovery of this posture, which the popes have always used in their private chapel. Meanwhile, the Pope urges that even when priest and people are separated on opposite sides of the altar, a cross be placed on the altar to allow all to focus on the Cross and not on themselves.

I still have a letter from an individual, written when I restored candles to the altar, objecting that this had been condemned by Vatican II. That was not the case, and now the Pope himself is reminding us of that. I have found and repaired the original cross from our high altar so that we can use it during Mass, as the Pope has desired. In the Pope's own words, "The cross, however much it might weigh, is not synonymous with misfortune, a disgrace to be avoided whenever possible.... The way of the Cross is in fact the only thing that leads to the victory of love over hate, of conversion over egotism, of peace over violence. Seen as such, Lent is truly an occasion of strong contemplative commitment and spirituality drawn from the grace of Christ."

February 17, 2008

THE TURKISH BELL TOLLS

The Transfiguration is celebrated on the sixth of August, but an account of it is also proclaimed as the liturgical Gospel in Lent, because it was a way in which the Lord prepared Peter, James, and John for the Crucifixion. These were the same apostles who would be with the Lord as He sweat blood the night before His death. Immediately after His Transfiguration, Christ would cure an epileptic suffering a violent seizure at the foot of the mountain: glory and agony within a few hours.

The unearthly light that shone from Christ on the mountaintop strengthened the apostles for when they would watch the sky grow dark on Good Friday. Even so, the apostles still would not fully understand why Christ had to die: when Our Lord told them that He must go to Jerusalem and "be lifted up," Peter said He would not allow it. What the Fisherman meant as a brave act of love, Jesus said was the work of the Evil One using Peter: "Get behind me, Satan" (Matt. 16:23).

Satan uses people in attempts to block God's plan, fooling and flattering them to use their power and talent to obscure the radiance of God. Sometimes he does this through individuals, and other times through political movements and false religions. One vivid example was the Siege of Belgrade in 1456.

Following the fall of Constantinople to the Muslims and the desecration of the world's largest church, Hagia Sophia (Holy Wisdom), the Ottoman Turks had worked their way into Europe, hoping to conquer Rome. Pope Callixtus III saw the Devil's work here, and summoned the brilliant Franciscan St. John of Capistrano, seventy years old, to crusade against the foe. At a meeting in Frankfurt, the friar found the Germans and Austrians too indifferent to take up arms, so he enlisted the Hungarian general John Hunyadi, and both of them, riding into battle against great odds, lifted the siege of Belgrade and delayed Muslim progress into Europe by about sixty years.

Hunyadi brandished a sword and Capistrano a more powerful crucifix. These great crusaders died shortly afterward from contagion. The Pope had ordered church bells to be rung at noon before the start of the conflict. News of victory reached Rome on the feast of the Transfiguration, so the Holy Father made it a universal feast. Moreover, he ordered that church bells be rung at every noonday.

In 1956, Pope Pius XII invoked the "Turkish Bell" as a summons to a crusade of prayer for oppressed Christians in Communist East Europe and China. The terror that stalks our world now, and would seek to block Christ, is diabolic and can be attributed to poor social conditions and economic deprivation only by the naïve or the cynical. Christ knew His enemy when He said, "Get behind me, Satan." Today there is great need for the bell to ring and move us to prayer and action.

March 1, 2015

SATAN'S ENEMY

In the Transfiguration, Christ showed that everything must center on Him to be of right service to humanity. Moses, representing the law and social order, defers to Him, as does Elijah, representing the intellect and the spiritual order. The Church recounts this in Lent, because Jesus revealed His glory in preparation for the Crucifixion.

Christ's glory sheds light on His three temptations in the wilderness. Satan tested Him to see if He would succumb to the deceits of secularism (turning stones to bread, as though matter were the only thing that really matters) and power (control of governments in exchange for cooperating with evil) and fantasy (attaining celebrity by flouting the laws of nature).

The Catholic Church is, as Pope John Paul II said, "expert in humanity." Satan's chief enemy is the Church, for this is Christ alive in the world. From hard experience the Church knows the temptations of secularism (reducing Christianity to philanthropic humanism), clericalism (bartering supernatural grace for social power), and subjectivism (living in a parallel universe contemptuous of moral reality).

To succumb to these temptations is to die, both personally and institutionally. The latest figures show that those denominations that surrendered to "the spirit of the age" are vanishing. The liberal Protestant denominations are evaporating. One of their leaders has said that their numbers are dropping because their members are too well educated to have children. It is hardly intelligent to design one's own demise. Our social fabric will have to adjust to the disappearance of these groups, which for a long while defined the public face of society. At the same time, the Catholic Church continues to grow, and would have done so even more had not many Catholics themselves yielded to the three-fold temptations. In the most recently recorded year, 2007 to 2008, the number of Catholics worldwide increased by 19 million people. Priests increased from 405,178 to 409,166. Seminarians increased from 115,919 to 117,024. As in the religious orders, the growth is invariably in those where the Faith is kept.

In the early nineteenth century, Tocqueville predicted that one day, the only options in the United States would be Catholicism and unbelief. In the early twentieth century, Chesterton said, "every man would end up either in utter pessimistic skepticism or as a member of the Catholic creed." In a famous vision, St. John Bosco saw little boats tying up with the Barque of Peter. This September, the successor of Peter will speak in Westminster Hall on the very spot where St. Thomas More was sentenced to death (and eternal glory) for defending the papacy. This is not a time for self-satisfaction. It is a summons to Lenten penance for our own subtle dalliances with temptations against the Faith, in the hope that we may respond more faithfully to the work of saving souls.

February 28, 2010

"You Will Strengthen Your Brethren"

The meteorite that exploded over Russia's Ural Mountains a week ago had the force of thirty atomic bombs. It was the biggest such impact since an asteroid exploded over Tunguska, Siberia, in 1908 with a force more powerful than all the bombs — including the atomic ones — dropped in the Second World War. Such a force of nature, when we observe it in the sky passing safely by with breathtaking speed, can also be a sign of the beauty and brevity of all things.

So it was in "The Year of Three Popes," when the death of Paul VI was followed by the death of John Paul I just four weeks after his election, and then the election of John Paul II. Cardinal Confaloniere said of John Paul I, in the exquisite Latin for which he was famous: "He passed as a meteor which unexpectedly lights up the heavens and then disappears, leaving us amazed and astonished."

The impact of that Pope's sudden death seemed at the time to be immeasurably hurtful, and yet he made the way for many providential events. Now the gracious abdication of Pope Benedict XVI also amazes and astonishes. When he assumed the papacy, he knew the work would not be easy: "Pray for me, that I may not flee for fear of the wolves." Without histrionics or self-pity, he quietly took up his burden in the succession of St. Peter, to whom the Lord said, "Simon, Simon, Satan has desired to have you, that he may sift you as wheat. But I have prayed for you, that your faith fail not; and that when you are converted, you will strengthen your brethren" (Luke 22:31–32).

In many glorious ways, Benedict XVI has done just that. With unerring fidelity he has explained the sacred deposit of the Faith to its opponents, both cultured and uncultured, with patient eloquence and stunning insight. Many reforms in the Church's structure and the purification of abuses were his intense initiatives. Rather like St. Francis of Assisi going to meet with the caliph of Egypt clad only in simplicity, Benedict XVI refused to wear a bullet-proof vest when he went to Turkey, turning the anger of many to respect. A new reverence and beauty in worship has been his gift to the Church through his renewal of the sacred rites. His provision of an ordinariate for whole groups seeking full communion with the Church "amazed and astonished" many. Now, his renunciation of the Keys entrusted to him teaches the essence of the papacy as a stewardship that transcends the charism of any individual.

Officially, a Pope is Bishop of Rome, Vicar of Christ, Successor of the Prince of the Apostles, Supreme Pontiff of the Universal Church, Primate of Italy, Archbishop and Metropolitan of the Roman Province, Sovereign of the State of the Vatican City, Servant of the Servants of God. But to the world, this Pope has also been a very good Father.

February 24, 2013

WALKING IS BETTER THAN FLYING

Of the temptations to which Our Lord allowed Himself to be subjected, the most difficult to understand was the temptation to fly. Actually, wanting to fly is not all that peculiar, if by peculiar is meant unique or unusual. Everyone is tempted to fly. By that, I do not mean the impetus that drove Icarus and the Wright Brothers. No, Satan's flying is contempt for reality. Wanting everything my way is flying in the face of facts.

Jesus, who walked on water, could have flown if He had subjected His human nature to His divine nature. He walked on water to teach Peter something, not to impress him. Satan tempted Jesus with the baser use of His divinity, to be superhuman instead of supernatural, Superman instead of Savior. Our Lord's response was: "You shall not tempt the Lord your God" (Matt. 4:7).

Our world, and certainly our nation, is suffering a crucible of temptations. In many ways we have already succumbed to them, which is why great saints have called ours a "Culture of Death." Attitudes and even sometimes laws have flown against reality: vice is freedom, decadence is dignity, killing unborn children is righteous, the unnatural is natural, maleness and femaleness are not facts but moods, and marriage is whatever the ego wants it to be.

Ego … for the temptation to fly is the primeval sin of pride, living a lie, and pretending that the world made by God is the world reinvented by man. By refusing to fly, Jesus saved us from the degradation of acting like idiots in a world of nonsense. It was expressed well by Alice as she prepared to enter Wonderland: "If I had a world of my own, everything would be nonsense. Nothing would be what it is, because everything would be what it is isn't. And contrary wise, what is, it wouldn't be. And what it wouldn't be, it would. You see?"

Tragically, there are those now who do see it that way and want the world to be Wonderland. The late, lamented Justice Antonin Scalia summoned some of our national patrimony's most formidable common sense and elegant expressions of it, graced with scintillating wit, to say that positive laws are rooted in realities deeper than whim. While some other jurists lived in Wonderland, he lived in God's creation.

Even Justice Scalia could be astonished at the ways man succumbs to fantasy. Crossing Park Avenue on a bright spring day, he stopped in the middle of traffic when I told him that the Dalton Books chain, now gone, had classified a book by the Hemlock Society about how to commit suicide, under the category "Self-Improvement." By God's grace, he can smile now before the God of both justice and mercy, but I think he must also grieve that so many still in this world think that they can fly.

February 21, 2016

THE TEMPTATIONS OF THE CHURCH

The Spirit that "drove" Jesus into the desert to be tempted by Satan (Mark 1:12) is the Third Person of the Most Holy Trinity—the bond of love between God the Father and God the Son. Christ was tempted three times as an act of love to prepare His Church for three temptations that would assault her in every generation.

Satan tested Christ to figure out if He truly was divine: "If you are the Son of God ..." So Satan also tempts the Church, not to discern her holiness as the Body of Christ, but to test whether Christians will be faithful to that holiness.

Satan first tempts the Church to turn stones into bread: to reduce the Church to a human creature devoid of supernatural charisms. The Church is the world's greatest feeder of the poor, but unless she feeds souls, she is redundant in a materialist culture. Satan wants to replace Communion lines with bread lines, as if the Body of Christ were nothing more than temporal sustenance. But Christ is Our Savior and not our Philanthropist. "Unless you eat the flesh of the Son of man, and drink his blood, you shall not have life in you" (John 6:53).

Secondly, Satan tempts the Church to mock herself, as he wanted Jesus to jump from the pinnacle of the Temple and survive. This test will see whether Christians will take up the daily crosses of life with Christ in a broken world, or engage grace as a kind of New Age energy arrogated to ourselves without moral obedience to natural law. To fly against nature is to live in an unreal world, claiming to be Catholic without living as Catholics. Satan wants us to "take Communion" on our terms rather than "receive Communion" on Christ's terms. St. Paul would not fly that way:

"He who eats and drinks without discerning the body, eats and drinks to his own condemnation; and for this reason many of you are weak, and ill, and some have died" (1 Cor. 11:29–30).

Thirdly, the Church is tempted with earthly power. Cardinal Consalvi reminded Napoleon that the Church's power is not from earthly rulers. Pope Pius XII said that Stalin would be able to count the Church's divisions only after he died. The two Thomases, Becket and More, made similar remonstrances with their own blood. In the history of the Church, Judas was the first to accept a government grant in exchange for doing evil.

The Church is entering a time of severe testing, and she will be crucified through tortures greater than nails, for she will be jeered by journalists, patronized by politicians, and menaced by false messiahs. But in the end, the Church's despisers will hear severe words: "You could have no power at all against me, were it not given you from above; so he who delivered me to you has the greater sin" (John 19:11).

March 8, 2009

What Is "Genius"?

In classical Latin culture, a *Genius* was a guiding spirit given to individuals from birth (*gignere*), enabling them to have special insights. It can be confused with *ingenium*, a power from within, not one that is endowed from without. From the latter we get words such as "ingenious" and "engine." An engine is not a *Genius*, nor does *Genius* exactly mean today what it originally meant.

The shift from having a genius to *being* a genius was gradual. Milton speaks of genius as we know it in his *Eikonoklastes*. With the idealization of reason in the eighteenth century, talk spread of the genius of mankind and of men who were geniuses. But if there ever were geniuses in that age — such as Newton — they did not think of themselves as such. Newton thanked God for his calculations. Mozart did not describe himself as other than a craftsman — rather as Blessed Teresa of Calcutta called herself a pencil in the hand of God. It is unlike the brooding spirit of Beethoven, to whom people doffed their hats, giving birth to the Romantic Age. I confess to bias when I say it reached degenerate heights with Wagner's "beautiful moments, but awful quarter-hours."

Two geniuses, if you will, to whom I tip my hat in respect are Newman and Chesterton. But they would be amused should anyone imply that their gifts were inborn and not given. Chesterton knew that people ran the danger of the foundational sin for all other sins, which is Pride. He said that he became a Catholic in order to get rid of his sins. He had no doubt about what caused the Fall of Man because evidence was all around him: "Certain new theologians dispute original sin, which is the only part of Christianity which can really be proved."[5]

Chesterton roared with laughter at himself, whereas Newman would rather smile. Chesterton was like a big bass drum, whereas Newman was more like a violin, but neither had pretensions to being anything other than made of clay into which God had breathed life. Newman warned against the veneration of "knowledge for its own sake" because it substitutes specimens of mental brilliance for holiness, "arrogating for them a praise to which they have no claim."

Then came Newman's warning spoken to intellectuals in one of his lectures on the proper idea of a university: "Quarry the granite rock with razors, or moor the vessel with a thread of silk; then may you hope with such keen and delicate instruments as human knowledge and human reason to contend against those giants, the passion and the pride of man."[6]

March 16, 2014

---

[5] G. K. Chesterton, *Orthodoxy*, chap. 2
[6] John Henry Newman, *The Idea of a University*, discourse 5, section 9.

THE SEVEN "HELPS"

As there are seven days in the week, so are there seven helps that, if practiced each day of the week, dispose the soul to receive many graces from God. Lent is the best time of the year to try them.

1. First, rise in the morning immediately—which can be a mortification—and offer the first groggy moment to God by saying, "I will serve." Satan said, "*Non serviam*" (I will not serve). Conquer the weakness of the first frail moment by this "morning offering," and the rest of the day will be more available to God's plans.

2. Spend fifteen minutes reading a portion of the New Testament, and sometimes also some good spiritual reading, such as the life of a saint or one of the classic guides to spiritual formation.

3. Spend another fifteen minutes in prayer as a simple conversation with Our Lord. The best way to do this, if it is possible, is before the Blessed Sacrament in a church.

4. Attend Mass on a weekday in addition to the Sunday Obligation. The ideal is daily Mass, and in Manhattan this is easier to arrange than in the suburbs. There may be times when one is not disposed to receive Communion. Don't violate the need to confess serious sins before receiving Our Lord—but do not fret. Bear in mind: to assist at Mass just by being a prayerful presence, making a spiritual communion, can bestow many graces.

5. At noon, pray the Angelus or, in the Easter season, the Regina Caeli. These prayers are available in most prayer books. This

helps remedy what was lacking in the first part of the day, and sets the tone for the rest of the day.

6. Pray five decades of the Rosary. This can even be done while walking or on the subway, sanctifying those "loose moments," provided you can be recollected about the mysteries while safely navigating traffic.

7. Examine your conscience at the end of the day: Have I prayed today? Did I do my work well for God's glory, especially when it seemed boring or unimportant? Have I "mortified" myself, that is, have I practiced little disciplines to channel the energy of my lower passions for good results? This will lead to good and frequent confession.

As a pole vaulter has to begin with a lower bar, one should get into these holy habits gradually. You will find that, paradoxically, the more time you spend on these sources of grace in a busy day, the more time will be available. If you do not "have" the time, God will "give" it—and will even add some.

March 3, 2002

YOU ARE THERE

When Shakespeare imagined what young King Henry V might have said before the Battle of Agincourt a century and a half before, he wrote one of the most celebrated speeches never really spoken. Nonetheless, it expresses the pride and thrill of having been privy to a great event:

> And gentlemen in England now a-bed,
> Shall think themselves accurs'd they were not here,
> And hold their manhoods cheap whiles any speaks,
> That fought with us upon Saint Crispin's day.

The eyewitness accounts of those who walked with Christ and saw the things He did and heard the words He spoke may give the impression that the narrators had an advantage over us these two thousand years later. St. John spoke with reverential awe of "What was from the beginning, what we have heard, what we have seen with our eyes, what we have looked at and touched with our hands, concerning the Word of Life" (1 John 1:1). However, not one of the apostles, nor, for that matter, any human being, was at the beginning of everything. It is by God Himself that the creation of the world is revealed, and it is by God in Christ that we learn our purpose in the created order. As Christ, who has no beginning or end, but has also a human nature that does have a birth and death, He conflates eternity and time so that when we are united with His death and Resurrection in baptism, we are able mystically to be at the beginning of the world and at its end.

"He is before all things, and in him all things hold together" (Col. 1:17).

St. Paul was not there at the Resurrection, but Christ came to him on the Emmaus road, and ever afterward the apostle would say in both defense and boast that he had been born "out of time" (1 Cor. 15:8). During the forty days of Lent, the Church is there with the Lord, going up to Jerusalem in an actual way, and not merely reminiscing or imagining, as in a stage play. This is a particular gift of these Lenten weeks, but it is not confined to this season. Nor is it limited to one place.

The Holy Eucharist enables all worshippers to be with the Lord, anyplace in the world at any hour, attending at the same time His sacrifice on the Cross and His Paschal victory. St. Peter could say with holy pride, "We ourselves heard this utterance made from heaven when we were with him on the holy mountain" (2 Pet. 1:18). And while that is a sublime thing to be able to say, so can we rejoice as well, for we too hear a voice from heaven when we are with the Lord at the holy altar: "This is my Body. . . . This is my Blood."

March 23, 2014

Knowing and Unknowing

A staple of late-night television comedy is a man-on-the-street interview, revealing the pervasive ignorance of people about basic matters of life. Among Americans aged 18 to 24, almost 30 percent cannot identify the Pacific Ocean on a map. Nearly half do not know when Columbus came to America. More than half cannot locate India, and 85 percent could not find Iraq, though many of them think they know more about it than our commander in chief. The typical college graduate today could not pass a standard examination required for admission to high school a century ago. The young people of the richest and most powerful nation in the world rank ninth from the bottom of all the industrial countries in science and humanities.

In a large number of our universities, seniors actually do more poorly than freshmen on questions about general culture. This reminds one of the university president who said that his school was a storehouse of knowledge because the freshmen bring so much knowledge in and the seniors take so little out.

The first obligation of knowledge is to know God. In addition to penance and almsgiving, Lent is a time to grow in knowledge of the Faith. Knowledge of religion has declined along with cultural knowledge in general. Many people accept what are in fact misperceptions of Catholicism. There are those who do not want to know, but there are many others who do want to learn if only others would teach them. As patience is a virtue, we should use it in bringing inquirers of goodwill into a fuller understanding of the gospel, dispelling those mistaken notions that are stumbling blocks to conversion of souls.

Practical reason is perfected by knowledge, while wisdom raises this a notch by guiding speculative knowledge. Knowledge teaches the "what" of things, and wisdom teaches the "why." So information alone does not suffice to make right judgments. George Orwell reflected on how the ordinary citizen generally is wiser in practical matters than the intelligentsia. He wrote, "The average intellectual of the Left believed, for instance, that the war was lost in 1940, that the Germans were bound to overrun Egypt in 1942, that the Japanese would never be driven out of the lands they had conquered, and that the Anglo-American bombing offensive was making no impression on Germany."[7]

It is not falsely optimistic to think that ordinary people of common sense can grasp the truths of holy religion, once they are given the facts, and it is not falsely pessimistic to assume that the educated despisers of religion will reject the facts in order to sustain their personal theories. But true wisdom can guide both, and that requires the gift of awe, which is the "holy fear" of which the Psalmist speaks: "The fear of the Lord is the beginning of wisdom" (Ps. 111:10; see Sir. 1:16).

February 24, 2008

---

[7] George Orwell, "Notes on Nationalism."

SMARTPHONES AND SOCIOPATHS

In normal usage, an idealist is someone with a lofty vision, possibly naïve but always noble in spirit. The term is more complicated in philosophy, but as a general category "idealism" means that mind takes precedence over matter, and reality cannot be separated from the mind's consciousness of it. The various schools of Idealism are subtler than that, but idealism makes the material world dependent on the self's perception of it. In the eighteenth century, a leading exponent of "subjective idealism" was the Anglo-Irish Protestant bishop George Berkeley, who lived for a while in the colony of Rhode Island. Dr. Samuel Johnson had no time for debating him and refuted Berkeley by kicking a rock.[8]

I doubt that many of the people absorbed in their "smartphones" through so much of the day, even while walking along the street or sitting in restaurants, engage much in philosophical discourse, but they are tottering on the brink of what philosophers would call *idealist epistemology*. Put simply: the universe belongs to them, and everything in it should be as they want it to be, with fact a form of feeling. Recently, when a conservative lecturer visiting a university told some harsh economic

---

[8] "After we came out of the church, we stood talking for some time together of Bishop Berkeley's ingenious sophistry to prove the nonexistence of matter, and that everything in the universe is merely ideal. I observed, that though we are satisfied his doctrine is not true, it is impossible to refute it. I never shall forget the alacrity with which Johnson answered, striking his foot with mighty force against a large stone, till he rebounded from it—'I refute it *thus*.'" James Boswell, *Life of Samuel Johnson*.

facts, undergraduates cried for psychotherapy. They had been emotionally bruised by kicking the rock of reality.

Adam and Eve were more than bruised when they ate of the Tree of the Knowledge of Good and Evil. They lost Paradise. Eating of the Tree meant arrogating to themselves the definition of reality. Taken to an extreme, that original sin of selfish pride produces the sociopath. That is a disordered antisocial personality like a psychopath, but the latter tends to be more erratic and violent with a probably genetic source for the condition. A sociopathic personality is shaped more by environment and circumstance.

Sociopaths are said to be about 4 percent of the population. They are not as easy to detect as psychopaths, and they smoothly charm their way well into influential positions in virtually all walks of life, often by means of glib eloquence. Along with their high intelligence, they are incapable of shame or guilt. They never apologize—for they think they have never done wrong. They exaggerate their achievements, dominate conversation, and manipulate people, and their narcissism makes them unable selflessly to love others, or to empathize even while claiming to do so. Above all, they are delusional, easily believing their own lies.

In His perfect humanity, Christ was the opposite of the antisocial, disordered personality. By His grace, His faithful apostles overcame their weaknesses and communicated His perfection. On the way to his own cross, which was not an invention of his imagination, the Prince of the Apostles wrote: "Make every effort to supplement your faith with virtue, virtue with knowledge, knowledge with self-control, self-control with endurance, endurance with devotion, devotion with mutual affection, mutual affection with love" (2 Pet. 1:5–7).

February 28, 2016

THE BATTLES OF BODY AND SOUL

Given the strengths and weaknesses of human nature, every day is a spiritual combat between our good intentions and our evil temptations. One of the subtlest of those temptations is to underestimate this struggle — supposing that a spiritual battle is less real than a physical battle. The fact is, while earthly warfare requires a full exercise of the natural virtues, the spiritual battle is even more intense, with consequences that extend beyond the limits of time and space. "For our struggle is not against flesh and blood, but against the rulers, against the powers, against the world forces of this darkness, against the spiritual forces of wickedness in the heavenly places" (Eph. 6:12).

It is inspiring to come across the lives of those who have acquitted themselves splendidly in both kinds of battle, earthly and spiritual. There is the example of the Navy SEAL and 2008 Medal of Honor recipient (posthumous), Michael Monsoor, whom the *New York Times* implied was a Muslim, although this devout Catholic regularly attended Mass before operations. We recently read about the canonization process for Father Vincent Capodanno, who gave his life in Vietnam as a navy chaplain. In April another Catholic chaplain will receive our nation's highest military honor — like Father Capodanno, posthumously. Both have also been declared Servants of God by the Church, meaning that their candidacy for sainthood is under official consideration.

Father Emil Kapaun was born in Kansas and was a parish priest before joining the army to serve in World War II and the Korean War. He died in a prisoner-of-war camp in 1951, seven months after having been taken prisoner by the Chinese. Not one of the military chaplains held prisoner by the North Koreans and the Chinese survived. Father Kapaun, though wounded and sick himself, risked his life to help his fellow prisoners under horrible conditions. Congress has finally approved the granting of the Medal of Honor, which is given for "conspicuous gallantry and intrepidity at the risk of life above and beyond the call of duty."

Not all heroes whose actions dignify the whole human race are saints. Sanctity is evidence of a different heroism: for heroic virtue, which marks the saint, is a constant habit of life, enabling the saint "to perform virtuous actions with uncommon promptitude, ease and pleasure from supernatural motives and without human reasoning, with self-abnegation and full control over his natural inclinations."[9]

Harry Truman said he would rather have the Medal of Honor than be president. In a loftier reference, Charles Péguy said, "Life holds only one tragedy, ultimately: not to have been a saint."

Even the most revered honor a people can bestow cannot match what awaits the victors of spiritual combat, and in that struggle all of us are enlisted and strive for "a crown that will never perish" (1 Cor. 9:25).

March 3, 2013

---

[9] Joseph Wilhelm, "Heroic Virtue," *Catholic Encyclopedia*, vol. 7 (New York: Robert Appleton Company, 1910).

THE TRANCE OF GOD

There are no throwaway lines in the Bible. All the words and phrases are there for a reason, even those long chronologies, which we may be inclined to skip over—until we realize that they are the record of our spiritual DNA, tracing the whole drama of God's guidance of human history.

We should pay special attention to words of rare usage, for their occurrence indicates a subtle meaning that we may miss. One instance is the Hebrew word *tardema*, meaning "sleep," which appears in the Old Testament only seven times. It is different from ordinary sleep, for it is a spiritual torpor—a "deep sleep"—obliterating all earthly senses, so that the intellect will not be overwhelmed by some great thing God is doing. The Greek word commonly translating *tardema* is the source of our "ecstasy." A *tardema* overcame Adam as woman was being formed from him, and Abram fell into a *tardema* when God prepared to connect with human events by making a covenant with the Jews. This coma-like state is the sort of trance that overcame Peter, James, and John at the Transfiguration on the mountain that is traditionally thought to be located at Tabor.

The point is that God takes the initiative and gently prepares mortals for what otherwise would be a traumatic shock at encountering another dimension of existence. Even with that conditioning, the three apostles were astonished when they came out of the stupor. Peter sort of babbled because, says St. Luke, "he did not know what he was saying" (9:33). God the Father was then heard: "This is my chosen Son; listen to Him" (9:35).

It is through Christ that the larger life of heaven becomes intelligible. To try to make sense of God on our own results in self-projection, to which the thousands of religious sects invented by mere human agency in our world attest. Left to his own logic, Peter wanted to enshrine the Logos, which is Jesus, as part of a trio, on par with Moses and Elijah. But after the Transfiguration, which Aquinas called the greatest of miracles before the Resurrection, Jesus "was found alone" (Luke 9:36). There is only one God, and we encounter Him in the Second Person of the Holy Trinity. "He who has seen me has seen the Father" (John 14:9).

The Holy Spirit graciously induces the deep sleep of the senses so that when human consciousness awakes, it does not confuse the divine Logos with human logic. The deep sleep that attends an encounter with God is different from biological fatigue, intensified by mental strain, such as the sleep that overcame the same three apostles in the Garden of Olives during Christ's agony. The small disciplines and penances of Lent help to move us from moral slumber to a deeper consciousness of God. Earthly dreams are fantasies, but what God shows us when He detaches us from earthly distractions awakens the soul.

March 7, 2010

LIKE LIGHT APPEARING

At the church door last Sunday, I inquired of various visitors where they were from. Some of the answers: Tokyo, Berlin, Moscow, Johannesburg, London, Marseilles. Then there were our own nationals, from Winston-Salem, Austin, Seattle, and other places beyond the typical Manhattanite's geographical vision. To have all of them worshipping "with the angels and saints" with us illustrates the dictum that the Catholic Church is too universal to be merely international.

The United Nations is international, but it does not extend into eternity, even though some of the speeches there might give that impression. Philanthropic organizations may be international in their good works, but the best of them cannot comfort the souls in Purgatory. And even the most prosperous international corporations cannot purchase the merits of the saints in glory.

The Catholic Church is not limited to time and space. As the Church Militant, she does cover the globe we live on, but as the Church Expectant she encompasses the holy souls in Purgatory preparing for the Beatific Vision, and as the Church Triumphant she counts in her ranks all the saints "like stars appearing."

Our Lord gave Peter and James and John a glimpse of this when He appeared with Moses and Elijah on Mount Tabor. There are those who glibly suggest that "catholic" means universal only in the international sense. One can be Catholic, though, only by confessing the same true Faith proclaimed by the saints at all times and in all places, as St. Vincent of Lerins famously put it.

This high claim shatters spiritual provincialism, by which I mean that kind of trendiness that trims belief to the assumptions of one's own generation. As Dean Inge said, he who marries the spirit of the age soon becomes a widower. And Chesterton reminded self-conscious progressivists that the Catholic Church "is the only thing that frees a man from the degrading slavery of being a child of his age."[10]

Catholicism is the only real cosmopolitanism because it is not limited to this fraction of the cosmos, and it is the only authentic sophistication because its "Sophia" is, as Newman taught, "the clear, calm, accurate vision and comprehension of the whole course, the whole work of God."[11]

Recently, as seems to happen routinely around Lent, a film producer made himself the laughingstock of archaeologists by claiming to have discovered the tomb of Christ—which he also claimed contained proof that Our Lord lived and died a bourgeois, like the rest of men. This sort of hoax seeks to affirm for us that the little world in which we live is the only world. The man who publicized the most recent iteration of this "discovery" does not appear to have adjusted to his own world well: he has been married five times and belongs to the Mars Society—an organization devoted to migration to another planet. Yet, the media salivate after these hoaxes, as though they defined the very frontiers of science and revealed our certain destiny. It is a degrading slavery to fall for such parlor tricks, and we hope that Lent saves many from such servitude.

March 11, 2007

---

[10] G.K. Chesterton, "Why I Am a Catholic."
[11] John Henry Newman, "Wisdom, as Contrasted with Faith and Bigotry."

WITH HIM ON THE HOLY MOUNTAIN

The same Jesus who was transfigured in glory on the mountain did a very earthy thing in using a whip to expel the moneychangers from the Temple. In the early weeks of Lent the Church recounts both as a reminder that God came into the world to change it. Christ's glory is displayed that "you might be partakers of the divine nature," but that glory is contingent upon our "having escaped the corruption that is in the world through lust" (2 Pet. 1:4).

As Jesus led Peter and James and John up the mountain, so He leads us up to glory, like the priest about to ascend the altar steps in the older form of the Mass: *Introibo ad altare Dei* (I will go unto the altar of God). That brush with divinity at the Transfiguration, enveloped by a cloud, is a preparation for the conflict between splendor and horror at the foot of the mountain. Pope Leo the Great explains how Our Lord was strengthening the apostles for the Crucifixion to come.

The kind of life that forgets God's glory becomes depressed, despite attempts to put on a veneer of happiness — like Cole Porter's song "Down in the Depths on the Ninetieth Floor." This does not mean that Christ saves us from conflicts. His followers must enter this world's gravest conflicts, but the consolation of His glory saves them from being psychologically conflicted. Having led the three apostles up the mountain, He leads them down. More help is needed going down than going up. This is a fact of mountaineering, and it is a fact of life itself. The same three apostles who witnessed Our Lord's glorious Transfiguration on the mountain attended His agony in the garden. By guiding the apostles down the mountain, Christ was instructing them in the virtue of the faith they would need for the trials ahead.

While there are more Catholics in the United States now than ever before, many of that number are immigrants and converts. One out of every ten Americans is a former Catholic. Excuses cannot conceal the fact that these people stumbled on the difficult path down from the summit of consolations. As Chesterton said: "Christianity has not been tried and found wanting; it has been found difficult and not tried."[12]

By being faithful, one proves Newman's maxim: "A thousand difficulties do not make one doubt."[13] It is too glib to speak of "losing" faith. Bernanos said pointedly, "Faith is not a thing which one 'loses,' we merely cease to shape our lives by it."[14]

Our Lord prayed that Peter's faith would not fail so that he might strengthen the brethren (Luke 22:32). Peter did precisely that to the end of his life:

"We did not follow cleverly devised myths.... We ourselves heard this voice from Heaven while we were with him on the holy mountain" (2 Pet. 1:16, 18).

March 15, 2009

---

[12] G.K. Chesterton, *What's Wrong with the World?*, pt. 1, chap. 5.
[13] John Henry Newman, *Apologia pro Vita Sua*, chap. 5.
[14] Georges Bernanos, *Diary of a Country Priest*.

"HAVE I BEEN SO LONG
WITH YOU, PHILIP?"

Stupidity is not ignorance. There is no cure for stupidity, but knowledge cures ignorance. Benjamin Franklin said there is no shame in ignorance, as long as you are willing to learn. This is the meaning of Alfred North Whitehead's dictum: "Not ignorance, but ignorance of ignorance, is the death of knowledge." Jesus gently prodded Philip: "Have I been so long with you, Philip, and do you still not know me?" (John 14:9). In the glory of the Resurrection, He asked the men on the Emmaus road how it was that they did not understand all that the prophets had written. In each instance, He patiently went on to explain.

I am not habitually speechless, but I find myself almost tongue-tied at the number of sane and intelligent people who take seriously the claims of the popular novel *The Da Vinci Code*. Discounting the self-deluded who use it as an excuse to "lose" the faith they never truly had, the situation points up the deep ignorance of many nominal Catholics. This is not an indictment. It is a summons to knowledge.

The United States Conference of Catholic Bishops has a new website designed to help save people from the gossamer bliss that comes from the anesthetic effects of ignorance. The *Da Vinci* book creates a fantasy about Mary Magdalene while claiming to base this on serious research. It develops a half-baked version of the heresy of Arius, who was more erudite, if less entrepreneurial, than the novel's author. The book makes ridiculous and anachronistic speculations about the emperor Constantine and the Christian creed. All this is exposed on the bishops' website and is treated at even greater length in various pamphlets and books by other writers who have made something of a cottage industry out of showing the delicacy of the novel's familiarity with history.

I suppose it is to be expected that a generation, the majority of whose college seniors cannot identify Lincoln or Churchill, might confuse St. John and St. Mary Magdalene. One can only hope that when a best-selling novel flaunts ignorance to a pyrotechnical degree, readers will realize how easily they are duped and how much they must learn. Lent is an appropriate time for such learning.

G. K. Chesterton devoted a book, called *The Thing*, to the mystery of Catholicism. Anyone who allows his brain a little exercise from time to time will face the fact that the Catholic Church has been the most important "Thing" in the annals of civilization. But if it is only a "Thing," and not Christ among us, it will haunt to distraction. Catholicism haunts the minds of men as the Ethical Culture Society and Anti-Vivisection Society do not. Haunted men do not write books about albino Unitarian assassins. The whole world was haunted until it was inspired by the Holy Spirit, who leads into all truth.

We are free to remain ignorant, as Pontius Pilate preferred to do. It is only speculation, but he may have spent his retirement back in Italy reading some morbid novels.

March 19, 2006

PIRATES

St. Paul knew from personal experience how difficult it would be for people of various cultures to understand why Jesus had to be crucified. For the more religiously disposed, whose most inspired matrix of belief was Judaism, the very suggestion of a crucified Messiah would be a scandal, while the more theoretical thinkers, none of whom were greater than the Greek philosophers, simply mocked the proposition.

Centuries later when the Koran was written, subtleties were abandoned altogether, and Sura 4 plainly says of Jesus, "They slew him not nor crucified him." The hard trials that our world is facing right now can, in large part, be traced to this denial of the Cross and the Resurrection, for it replaces Christ's atonement for human sin with a primitive understanding of salvation.

Exactly 229 years ago this month, when the Barbary pirates were menacing ships of the newborn United States off the coasts of Tunis and Algiers, Thomas Jefferson and John Adams met in London with a Muslim diplomat representing the dey of Algiers to inquire why his religion made his people so hostile to a new country that posed them no threat. They reported to Congress through a letter to John Jay, then secretary of foreign affairs, the ambassador's explanation that:

> Islam was founded on the Laws of their prophet, [and] that it was written in their Quran, that all nations who should not have acknowledged their authority were sinners, that it was their right and duty to make war upon them wherever they could be found, and to make slaves of all they could take as prisoners, and that

every Mussulman who should be slain in battle was sure to go to paradise.

Islam believes that Jesus was raised bodily to heaven and will return to earth at the end of time. It holds that if Jesus had been crucified, He would have died, and that would have been His end. The consequences of not understanding God's love, crowned and enthroned, albeit with thorns on a Cross, are vivid now in the horrors being inflicted on Christians in many places. For if God is pure will without reason, whose mercy is gratuitous and has nothing to do with any sort of moral covenant with the human race, then irrational force in His name is licit, and conscience has no role in faith. This is not the eccentric interpretation of extremists; it is the logical conclusion of the assertions in the Quran itself.

The true Word of God confounds any crude dismissal of the Cruci-fixion as though it were a denial, and not a proof of divine power. Jesus spoke of Himself as the true Temple, which, if destroyed, would be raised in three days. "Therefore, when he was raised from the dead, his disciples remembered that he had said this, and they came to believe the Scripture and the word Jesus had spoken" (John 2:22).

March 8, 2015

LAETARE, IERUSALEM

Christ fell three times beneath the Cross. He also got up three times. We fall all the time. The whole human race fell in its first generation. The Fall of Man is misery writ large. What matters for our eternal happiness is that we get up again. So a great saint said, oblivious to his own sanctity, "Not all the saints started well, but they finished well."

The Fourth Sunday of Lent is a chance to reflect on progress and stumbles, to make an inventory of body and soul, and to get up and start again. We are not the ones to judge if we are making progress. Only God can judge that. But it is sufficient that we don't stay down. Discouragement is a chief strategy of the Prince of Lies. He plays on human pride in two ways, alternating between the presumptuous posture that thinks we are doing fine, and the defeatist posture that assumes we are hopeless. The fable of the tortoise and the hare is a pleasant pagan analogy of this. Aesop told it some six centuries before St. Paul spoke of enduring the race, and the word he uses for the race, *agonizomai*, is the Greek word for "contest," which we dramatize into our term "agony." He is quite cheerful about it, really, and what he emphasizes is that there is hope of a great victory, provided we realize that the spiritual journey is more like a marathon than a sprint. In fact, people who only sprint in life's journey will enjoy an occasional spiritual "rush," but they will be disappointed in time of trial.

This Fourth Sunday is called Laetare because, like Gaudete Sunday in Advent, it is provided to encourage the runner not to give up. "Rejoice, Jerusalem." The penitential tone is lessened, and a hint of the Resurrection seeps in. As Pierre Abelard wrote:

Now, in the meanwhile, with hearts raised on high,
We for that country must yearn and must sigh,
Seeking Jerusalem, dear native land,
Through our long exile on Babylon's strand.

I recently read of a television personality who deals with bouts of depression by hanging upside down. Sometimes the same people who do that sort of thing mock the Church's precepts for mortifying the senses. Hanging upside down may actually be helpful for the bones and the brain. I do not know. But it seems to me more fitting for bats than for saints. St. Peter was crucified upside down, but not because he was depressed. His was a joy that is promised to all those who follow the Lord.

"Wherefore seeing we also are compassed about with so great a cloud of witnesses, let us lay aside every weight, and the sin which so easily besets us, and let us run with patience the race that is set before us" (Heb. 12:1).

March 18, 2007

The Hatred Whose Name We Dare
Not Speak (Genocide)

The fine Latinity of Laetare Sunday means to be joyful, and as the mother of civilization, the Holy Church encourages her children to keep pressing on toward the Easter prize. Just as Eskimos and Arabs have many words for snow and sand, the ample resources of Latin give us more than one word for rejoicing. There is *gaude*, from which we get gaudy celebration, so in the somber days of Advent we have Gaudete Sunday. *Gaude et laetare, Virgo Maria.* We shall sing that at Easter, but *laetare* creeps in on the Fourth Sunday of Lent.

Back to Greek: I indulge *apophasis*, which means saying that I am not going to say what I am going to say, to remark that there is no need to mention, in this rose-colored time of Lent, that our brothers and sisters in the Faith in Iraq and Syria are suffering terribly. The Pope and various national leaders have used the word that our chief executive will not pronounce: genocide. If a hapless youth is shot on one of our city streets, it is front-page news, but the beheading of Christian infants in the Middle East hardly gets a comment.

Our current president has told the United Nations that the future must not belong to those who slander the Prophet of Islam, and he makes a habit of saying that terror attacks have "nothing to do with Islam." Our government has purged any reference to Islam from military and intelligence training manuals, and immigration policies favor Islam to the extent that, so far this year, 602 Muslim immigrants have been granted asylum while only 2 Christians have. Meanwhile, Christianity is being eradicated in the Middle East, and churches and monasteries destroyed.

The Knights of Columbus have received more than 25,000 names for a petition asking the secretary of state to designate the systematic mass murder of Christians by the Islamic State (ISIS or ISIL) as genocide. Iraqi and Syrian Christians fear going to refugee camps because they may be killed by Muslim "hit squads."

This transcends all the issues that transfix political candidates now seeking to repair what is broken in our nation. We are in the predicament that some of our Founding Fathers faced as they tried to make sense of what was to them an obscure and exotic religion that was damaging American commerce and compromising the new nation's sovereignty: pirates employed by such Muslim Barbary states as Algiers were enslaving thousands of Americans.

In a recent talk to the Islamic Society of Baltimore—which the FBI warned him had radical allegiances—President Obama said that Thomas Jefferson and John Adams had copies of the Quran. He neglected to say that they were not seeking spiritual edification. They were trying to anatomize what was to them a fount of cruelty and an engine of hysteria. Our Lady knew that kind of mentality when she watched her Son dragged through the streets.

March 6, 2016

SALVATION OR NARCISSISM

To approach Holy Week is to approach the core of reality. The Incarnation of Christ, by which the divine Second Person of the Holy Trinity also became a real man, contradicts the mood of oriental religions that seek to escape the body. In a problematic world, the limited human intellect prefers excarnation to incarnation. Incarnation makes solemn and magnificent moral demands on the realist.

The tragedy of the human condition is its failure to be really *real*. Holiness is the realization of what we are supposed to be. It does not happen by overcoming the body; it happens by overcoming the ego. This is the "one-ness with God" intended by Christ in His agony in the garden: "And now I am no more in the world, but these are in the world, and I come to thee. Holy Father, keep through thine own name those whom thou hast given me, that they may be one, as we are one" (John 17:11).

People focused on themselves seek therapy instead of salvation. Religion, or its substitutes in the form of pop psychology and narcissistic culture, is to them just an emotional attempt to redesign nature to fit one's illusions. Therapy replaces grace, and then selfishness inverts natural law. When this infects Catholics, self-absorption replaces the worship of God, and Catholic Light becomes Catholic-Lite.

As the writer David Brooks puts it, "Here, sins are not washed away. Instead, hurt is washed away. The language of good and evil is replaced by the language of trauma and recovery. There is no vice and virtue, no moral framework to locate the individual within the cosmic infinity of the universe. Instead there are just the right emotions—*Do you feel good about yourself?*—buttressed by an endless string of vague bromides about how special each person is, and how much we are all mystically connected in the flowing river of life."[15]

His rhetoric about an infinite universe is imprecise, for the universe is a creature and therefore finite, but he hits precisely on the condition that H. Richard Niebuhr detected in the Liberal Protestantism of the 1930s: "A God without wrath brought men without sin into a kingdom without judgment through the ministrations of a Christ without a Cross."[16]

The spiritual narcissist cannot exist in the Heavenly Jerusalem because he can look only at himself instead of at God. Hilaire Belloc said, "A man who does not accept the Faith writes himself down as suburban." Suburbanized Catholicism has nothing to do with where we live. It is the narcissism that rejects the Heavenly City by wanting a therapist instead of a savior. Holy Week shows the world the Passion to save it from such indignity.

March 28, 2004

---

[15] David Brooks, "Hooked on Heaven Lite," *New York Times*, March 9, 2004, https://www.nytimes.com/.

[16] H. Richard Niebuhr, *The Kingdom of God in America*, chap. 5.

EVIDENCE OF BIRTH

The Belgian priest and physicist Monsignor Georges Lemaître died in 1966 after receiving news that his theory of the birth of the universe—which he called the "hypothesis of the primeval atom"—had been confirmed by the discovery of cosmic microwave background radiation.

Albert Einstein had been slow in coming around to Lemaître's hypothesis of an expanding universe, now popularly called the "Big Bang"—a term that was first meant in subtle mockery. But then he commended it to further research. Just weeks ago, scientists published evidence of the almost instantaneous expansion of all matter from an infinitesimal particle. The scale and volume of this stuns the human mind. But at least, if the mind cannot grasp this, it can acknowledge it, along with the fact that there was no time or space before that "moment." It fits well with the record in Genesis—where the voice of the eternal and unlimited God utters light and all consequent creatures into existence.

Here one must be careful in attributing to physical science an explanation of the "why" as well as the "how" of creation. Theology—equally the highest science—must not confuse itself with physics. As I have mentioned, Cardinal Baronius said in the sixteenth century, "The Bible was written to show us how to go to heaven, not how the heavens go." In a moment of unguarded enthusiasm in 1951, Pope Pius XII said that Lemaître's theory proved the existence of God. He humbly backed off when Lemaître told him that a physical hypothesis could do no such thing.

At the same time, no human hypothesis can tell us what God alone can reveal: that He made the world and all that is in it for His delight.

When we delight God by doing His will, His delight infuses His sentient creatures with joy. The composer Gustav Holst may have employed some fanciful theology (theosophy) in giving personalities to seven planets in his famous symphony, but the "jollity" of Jupiter is a compelling metaphor for the joy of the saints.

Laetare Sunday in the middle of Lent is not so much an interruption of the penitential season as it is an encouragement not to lose the focus of Lent and of life itself on the joy that God offers us in Heaven — where there is no time or space, as it was before the world began.

The Church goes "up" to Jerusalem in an earthly sense as a metaphor for moving toward the Heavenly Jerusalem, which "has no need of sun or moon to shine on it, for the glory of God gives it light, and its lamp is the Lamb" (Rev. 21:23). This is a wonder more daunting and challenging than the most abstruse hypotheses of the most brilliant physical scientists. It moves beyond the pleasure of speculation into the purest happiness of encounter. "Rejoice, O Jerusalem; and come together all you that love her."

March 30, 2014

MAKING THE BEST OF OUR DAYS

Laetare Sunday, marking the midpoint in the path to Easter, is also a road sign to our eternal home. This is not escapism: to know that Heaven is the goal is a formula for making the best of our days on earth. To be "partway there" means that there is a there, unlike Gertrude Stein's opinion of Oakland, California, that "there is no there there."

Christ walked "up to Jerusalem" in order to go up to Heaven, and His cleansing of the Temple in Jerusalem was His sign that He would also cleanse human minds and hearts to "go up" with Him. The mind and heart, that is, the intellect and will, compose the soul, with the intellect consisting of the imagination and reason. Our Lord cleanses by being "the Way, the Truth, and the Life." As the Way, He guides the imagination to a perception of eternity. As the Truth, He aids the reason to grasp the truth. As the Life, He guides the will to choose life. Just as corrupt men had defiled the Temple, Satan corrupts the soul: he would have us imagine things hellish instead of heavenly, and rationalize lies, and choose death. Baptism cleanses the soul of these corruptions, and confession is a sort of regular maintenance for the cleansed soul.

Jesus knows of Heaven — "In my Father's house are many mansions" (John 14:2) — and so He becomes angry when the Temple, as an earthly sign of Heaven, is turned into a bourgeois marketplace. And that anger is also kindled when He sees sin defiling the human soul. As St. Paul says, "Do you not know that your bodies are temples of the Holy Spirit?" (1 Cor. 6:19). Christ's wrath is always righteous because it focuses on evil. He never loses His temper: He finds it to cleanse corruption.

Divine anger is not a weakness of God, but a sign of His perfection. It is a sign of God's love for those whom He does not want to lose along the way. Another sign of God's love is His tears, as when He wept for Lazarus and for all Jerusalem that would be gathered to Him. As His sons and daughters, we have the gift of holy anger, which is destructive only when we "lose our temper." The solution is to find it, and that we do when we confess our sins, directing our anger at the Prince of Lies. Along with this confession comes the gift of tears, which man alone among all creatures can shed, for the human being is not made for this world alone: "Our immortality / Flows thro' each tear—sounds in each sigh."

Divine wrath saves us from losing our temper and wasting our tears. "The wrath of God is revealed from Heaven" (Rom. 1:18). And it is revealed from Heaven so that we might arrive there.

March 22, 2009

A Benevolent Plan for Each Soul

Helen Hayes, a devout Catholic and the daughter in a long Irish family line, died in 1993 on the feast of St. Patrick. Her acting career spanned nearly seventy years. She was a teenager when she performed in the play *Dear Brutus*, whose author, Sir J. M. Barrie, also wrote *Peter Pan*. The play is about people who enter a magic garden to see what they might have become had they chosen different paths in life. The title is from Shakespeare's *Julius Caesar*, where Cassius plots: "The fault, dear Brutus, is not in our stars, but in ourselves, that we are underlings."

Blaming the stars for what happens to us was the essence of Greek tragedy, where the hero is a victim of forces beyond his control. That word "tragedy" entered English usage only around 1500. Christians believe in providence rather than in fate: for each soul, God has a benevolent plan, which we are free to accept or reject. Classical tragedy, on the other hand, has little if anything to do with moral choices, and the pagan gods were moved more by whim than by justice.

Without Christ, culture lapses into the old paganism, blaming "bad luck" or "karma." The one true God does not throw tantrums like the gods of the pagan pantheon. Because the Jews believed in a just God, they asked Jesus if some people slain by Pontius Pilate were being punished for sin. Then Jesus mentions a natural disaster that killed eighteen people (Luke 13:1–5).

Addressing this recently, Pope Benedict XVI said: "Jesus invites us to interpret these facts differently, connecting them with conversion: misfortunes, sorrowful events, should not arouse curiosity in us or a seeking of people presumed to be guilty, but they must be occasions for reflecting, for overcoming the illusion of pretending to live without God, and for reinforcing, with the Lord's help, the commitment to change our life."[17] I am not to blame if I get hit by a brick, but I am accountable for how I respond to the brick and whoever threw it.

There are two sides to fatalism: pessimism, which expects the worst, and optimism, which presumes the best. "Whoever thinks he is standing secure should take care not to fall" (1 Cor. 10:12). In contrast to both, is the virtue of hope, which trusts that God will not fail us if we do not fail Him. The Crucifixion of the world's one innocent man was the worst crime in history, but it was not a meaningless tragedy, because it brought good out of evil. Those who are "crucified with Christ" through daily trials are not tragic heroes, but saints. St. Basil says: "Here is man's greatness, here is man's glory and majesty: to know in truth what is great, to hold fast to it, and to seek glory from the Lord of glory."[18]

March 14, 2010

---

[17] Benedict XVI, Angelus message, March 7, 2010.
[18] St. Basil, Homily 20 *De humiliate*, 3.

"He Who Believes Shall Be Saved"

Maewyn Succat did not have an easy time embracing the Faith. Although his father, Calpurnius, was a deacon, Maewyn indulged a spirited youthful rebellion against what he had been taught, and it was only after being kidnapped by superstitious people called Druids that he realized the difference that Christianity makes in the souls of men and the character of cultures. This was in the fifth century, and Maewyn, probably born in the Cumbria part of England near the Scottish lands, was roughly contemporary with the bishop Augustine in North Africa, who watched the decay of the Roman Empire. Maewyn eventually became a bishop in Rome, where Pope Celestine I renamed him Patricius, which means "Father of his people." His people were to be in the land of Eire, where he had suffered in virtual slavery.

Patrick was neither the first nor the only man to bring the gospel to Ireland. Foundations were also laid by such missioners as Palladius, Ciarán of Saighir, Auxilius, Secundinus, and Iserinus. One reason Patrick was sent to Ireland was to stem the spread of the Nestorian heresy, which misrepresented the hypostatic union of Christ as true God and true man. A couple of centuries later, Nestorians in the East would influence Mohammed's misunderstanding of Christ. Patrick was not subtle when it came to the truth: "That which I have set out in Latin is not my words but the words of God and of apostles and prophets, who, of course, have never lied. He who believes shall be saved, but he who does not believe shall be damned. God has spoken."[19]

---

[19] St. Patrick, *Letter to the Soldiers of Coroticus* 20.

If Patrick, whom the archdiocese of New York is privileged to invoke as its patron, could witness what has become of his feast in the streets of our city, he might think that the Druids were having their revenge. He certainly would decry the notion that his feast was merely a celebration of an ethnic identity that was not his, or of a conviviality not rooted in Christian moral reason. This Saint Patrick's Day, Maewyn/Patricius would bond more instinctively with the beheaded and crucified martyrs in the Middle East and Nigeria (whose official patron is Patrick) who are now spilling their blood for Christ, than with some revelers on Fifth Avenue spilling beer. There is a difference between martyrs and leprechauns.

This is not to dampen good spirits and rightful celebration, risky though they are in these forty days, when the shadow of the Cross looms larger daily. But it is a reminder of the cost of discipleship in a cynical culture, and of the heavy cost of succumbing to the threats of the morally bewildered — who with adolescent petulance long to intimidate the Church that carried the Gospel across the Irish Sea. Patrick said when he braved the dark pagan groves: "If I be worthy, I live for my God to teach the heathen, even though they may despise me."[20]

---

[20] Ibid., 1.

THE COURAGE TO CONTINUE

The annals are replete with the failures of famous figures. Although some accounts are embellished, Abraham Lincoln's setbacks are daunting. He lost his job and was defeated for the state legislature in 1832 and then failed in business. He had a nervous breakdown in 1836 and was defeated for Speaker of the Illinois House two years later. In 1843 his nomination for Congress failed, and he was defeated for the U.S. Senate in 1854 and 1858, between which he lost the nomination for the vice presidency.

That is only half of the picture. After disappointment in 1832, he was elected captain of the Illinois militia in the Black Hawk War. Following the failure of his business, he was appointed postmaster of New Salem and was twice elected to the state legislature. His law practice grew, and he was admitted to plead before the U.S. Supreme Court. His rejection for land officer in 1849 was followed by the offer of the governorship of the Oregon Territory, which he declined. He dusted himself off and was elected president in 1860.

Winston Churchill long struggled with his "Black Dog" of depression. His advocacy of the disastrous Gallipoli campaign in the First World War seemed to put him on the shelf of ruined men, and from then on he was often mocked, painting pictures to keep moral balance during his "Wilderness Years." Only because Lord Halifax demurred the premiership following Chamberlain's resignation did King George VI appoint Winston as a second choice in 1940. Early war defeats seemed overwhelming. The military occupation of Norway was a demoralizing calamity.

The point is that if one falls, one can get up again. Churchill said, "Success is not final, failure is not fatal: it is the courage to continue that counts." This counsel is more than the banal "positive thinking" of glib men. It is rooted in a genuine humility that is willing to be helped up by a conviction of Providence, rather than refusing to get up out of crippling pride. Still, such persistence was a specimen only of natural virtue. Great figures in history who perdured are not in the choirs of saints unless they have also employed the theological virtues of faith, hope, and love. Not all the great are saints, but all the saints are great. As I've mentioned before, Saint John Vianney said: "Not all saints started well, but all of them ended well."

In the Stations of the Cross we recollect: "Jesus falls a first time. Jesus falls a second time. Jesus falls a third time." That makes sense only if we also whisper: "Jesus gets up a first time. Jesus gets up a second time. Jesus gets up a third time." When the Antichrist tries to push us down, Christ can lift us up to life eternal. "Even if good people fall seven times, they will get back up. But when trouble strikes the wicked, that is the end of them" (Prov. 24:16).

March 22, 2015

THE SECRET OF JOY

The sociopath is the photographic negative of Christ, in whom we can see the Father. In the sociopath, we catch a glimpse of the Prince of Lies. The sociopath makes sorrow a contagion, while Christ spreads joy (cf. John 15:11) by giving Himself to us as "grace," which enables us to love. The sociopath cannot love because he is frozen within himself. The youthful Saul of Tarsus may have been a budding sociopath, destructive in his self-regard, but the Risen Christ changed all that. Sixty percent of the occurrences of the word "joy" in the New Testament are from St. Paul, who did not know its meaning before his conversion.

In Greek, "joy" and "grace" sound much the same, for *hara* is nurtured and perfected by *haris*. St. Paul says (2 Cor. 2:3ff) that "my joy is the joy of you all," and he urges us to save others from becoming "swallowed up with overmuch sorrow." That word "overmuch" is the craft of the King James translation and needs no updating in our conflicted world. In St. Paul, and in all the saints, is sensed the personality of Christ whom some adored and some scorned, but whom no one ever found manipulative. And not even His enemies found Him depressing.

By following Our Lord as He walks into the cauldron of the earthly Jerusalem, with its rampant pathologies, the Church also walks toward the heavenly Jerusalem, where all is joy, because all are looking at God instead of themselves.

"Be glad and rejoice for ever and ever for what I am creating, because I now create Jerusalem 'Joy' and her people 'Gladness.' I shall rejoice over Jerusalem and exult in my people. No more will the sound of weeping or the sound of cries be heard in her; in her, no more will be found the infant living a few days only, or the old man not living to the end of his days. To die at the age of a hundred will be dying young; not to live to be a hundred will be the sign of a curse. They will build houses and inhabit them, plant vineyards and eat their fruit" (Isa. 65:18–21).

March 21, 2010

HOUSE OF GRACE

One of the most redundant expressions in common use is "a living saint." There are no dead saints, though they pass through death. Saints living in our midst are just in the first stage of that process. Their liveliness is not just a spectacle to admire, but a model to follow.

In Holy Week, the Church follows Our Lord along the path He walked in history. The saints follow Him as their Savior from sin and death. When He healed the paralytic at the pool of Bethesda in Jerusalem, He warned him: "See, you are made well. Sin no more, so that something worse does not happen to you" (John 5:14). What could be worse than being paralyzed for thirty-eight years like that man? Worse than physical sickness is sickness of soul. Christ cures that in baptism and confession. A quadriplegic with a pure soul can attain eternal glory, when even an Olympic runner without divine grace cannot.

After He had healed the man, Jesus went into hiding, for He had not come to cure the flesh, but to cure the fatal contagion of mortality itself. In Passiontide, by an old tradition, the crucifix is veiled as a sign of this, and statues of saints are covered too, because Christ's followers do not walk abroad while He is in the shadows. This is not fanciful stage acting. It is the living history of which all of us are part. Formerly, many scholars, such as the cynical Alfred Loisy, thought St. John's description of the pool of Bethesda might have been inaccurate or misinterpreted, but very recently archaeologists uncovered the full splendor of the pool of Bethesda just as the Beloved Apostle described it. *Beth Chesda* is Hebrew for "House of Grace," and that grace was real and effective, not by the water in the pool but by the will of Christ, whose simple command cured a man.

The liturgical reliving of the Passion is different from nostalgia. A wit said that nostalgia is history after a few drinks. The solemn liturgies walk us through the events that open the gates to eternal life, and this aperture into eternity is as real as the Golden Gate that opened on the first Palm Sunday and the tombstone that rolled away on the first Easter. Passion Sunday this year is the first anniversary of the death of Pope John Paul II at 9:27 P.M. in the Apostolic Palace. The Vatican is still there, and John Paul's successor is there, serenely leading the flock as the newest successor of Peter. John Paul is no less alive now that he has gone, as he prayed, to the "House of the Father."

In these days, the Church prays for the catechumens about to enter the Church in the Easter Vigil, that they and all of us may give thanks for such great mysteries.

April 3, 2006

HUMILITY SIMPLIFIES

"All the way to Heaven is already Heaven," said St. Catherine of Siena —for those who follow Christ, who does not merely show the way but is the Way. It is also the case that all the way to Easter is already Easter for those who love the Lord, even in Lent. The Liturgy is an entrance into the mystery of eternity, which is why the feasts and fasts overlap and intersect. The Liturgy is not playacting, and those who think it is tend to turn the drama of salvation into didactic melodrama, replacing holy water with sand, and staging self-conscious "liturgical dancing" instead of the solemn rituals of the rubrics, and so forth. The mystery we enter through the Liturgy is real enough and does not need contrived mystification. Through ardent prayer the Church perceives real glimpses of Easter joy even in the midst of Lenten penance, just as Easter joy does not hide the Cross, through which the triumph over death was won.

In Lent there are glimpses of Easter joy in two feasts we call *solemnities* because of their importance: the solemnity of St. Joseph and the solemnity of the Annunciation. In St. Joseph's yes to God when he wed Our Lady, despite his bewilderment at the circumstances of her pregnancy, and in the Virgin Mary's yes to God, despite her own incomplete comprehension of what the Lord was doing, are seen the way to enter into heavenly joy on earth and know that "peace which passes all understanding" (Phil. 4:7). These feasts do not interrupt the tone of Lent. They keep it on course toward the goal of all living.

Pride complicates life, and humility simplifies it, and total humility attains spiritual perfection. Blessed Teresa of Calcutta had a formula for this: "Just give God permission." Once a soul "gives God permission" in confession and daily mortification of selfishness, God empowers the virtues to accomplish what He wants. The sublime consummation of this is in Our Lord's own obedience to His Father at the start of His holy agony: "Not my will but Thine be done" (Luke 22:42).

St. Bernardine of Siena considered how this works, with special reference to the model of St. Joseph: "There is a general rule concerning all special graces granted to any human being. Whenever the divine favor chooses someone to receive special grace, or to accept a lofty vocation, God adorns the person chosen with all the gifts of the Spirit needed to fulfill the task at hand."[21]

Dying with the ineffable consolation of Our Lord and Our Lady at his deathbed, St. Joseph is the patron saint of a holy death each of us prays for. He could claim the promise that each day of Lent both anticipates and already senses: "Good and faithful servant, enter into the joy of your Lord" (Matt. 25:21).

March 25, 2007

---

[21] St. Bernardine of Siena, Sermon 2.

Your Step Gets Firm and Sure

In 1943, just up the street from our church, in the Hotel New Yorker, the pioneer of electrical inventions, including alternating current, Nikola Tesla died in room 3327. He wrote: "With ideas it is like with dizzy heights you climb: At first they cause you discomfort and you are anxious to get down, distrustful of your own powers; but soon the remoteness of the turmoil of life and the inspiring influence of the altitude calm your blood; your step gets firm and sure and you begin to look—for dizzier heights."[22]

St. Peter obeyed Our Lord and got out of his fishing boat to take a step on the water. That first step, which must have seemed dizzying, made all the difference in the course of world history. The apostle James was in that boat and watched what happened. Later he would write: "Draw near to God, and he will draw near to you" (James 4:8). Taking the first step is an act of faith. Babies have faith enough in their thrilled parents to hold their hands as they bid them take the first step. From that step proceeds all the walks through life.

From time to time, one counsels a young person hesitant to take a first step: to accept a new job, or to propose marriage, or to seek the priesthood. The challenge can be intimidating in our culture, whose

---

[22] Nikola Tesla, "On Electricity" (address on the occasion of the commemoration of the introduction of Niagara Falls power in Buffalo at the Ellicot Club, January 12, 1897), *Electrical Review*, January 27, 1897, posted on the website of Twenty-First Century Books, http://www.tfcbooks.com/.

chief seduction is to find comfort and security. Nothing great or noble has been achieved by seeking safety. Jesus promised: "Seek first the Kingdom of God and his righteousness, and all these things will be given to you" (Matt. 6:33). That means taking the first step toward Jesus, and then He will step toward you. The surest way to make it up the staircase without tripping is to focus on the top landing. But it all begins with the first step.

The poet Horace said in the first book of his Odes: "*Carpe diem, quam minimum credula postero*"—roughly meaning: "Seize today and don't worry about tomorrow." That was about a generation before Jesus said in a Judean backwater: "Come, follow me." Today. The book of Numbers speaks of "journeying" nearly ninety times, and that journeying, which is a microcosm of the entire human experience, began with one first step.

In response to the credulous Cardinal de Polignac, who claimed that the martyr St. Denis had carried his decapitated head two miles, the caustic wit Marie Anne Marquise du Deffand said, "*Il n'y a que le premier pas qui coûte*" (It's the first step that counts).

By an incontestable logic, if we can manage just one first step toward Jesus, He will walk with us all the way to Easter and to Heaven itself.

March 13, 2016

THE SANHEDRIN TODAY

Christ performed miracles, or "signs," to explain His approaching death and Resurrection. He gave sight to the blind man (John 9) to describe the virtue of faith, by which we recognize the power of His victory over death.

He took the initiative in His approach to the blind man. This means, first, that faith comes from God and is not the invention of our wishful thinking. "In this is love: not that we have loved God, but that he loved us and sent his Son as expiation for our sins" (1 John 4:10). Secondly, faith requires obedience. Although the blind man could have washed in any water, Christ commanded that he wash in the Pool of Siloam. By doing so, the blind man conformed his will to God's, just as the leper Naaman washed in the Jordan according to Elisha's command, although he first objected that the rivers Abana and Pharpar in his native Syria were better, as rivers go.

Our limited reason may question the logic of God's commandments, but what matters is not logic but the Logos, the source of all logic. Jesus resolved this conflict between perception and the source of perception in his own human nature: "Not my will, but thine, be done" (Luke 22:42). When the blind man did God's will, he was changed: no longer an obsequious beggar but a winner in debate with the Pharisees. Defeated, the Pharisees could only try to get rid of him.

Pride blinds the heart to reality. Our Lord predicted that some would not believe, even "were one raised from the dead" (Luke 16:31). Moral blindness prefers impressions to facts. An example is the Holy Father's recent apostolic journey to Africa. On one occasion, Pope Benedict offered

Holy Mass in the presence of one million people. To the Pope's sorrow, some were killed or injured in a rush to get near him. But it seemed that much of the faithless media rushed to get away from him. They ignored the Pope's message of salvation and mocked his moral teaching.

On the subject of stemming disease by the use of contraceptives, the Pope was telling the obvious truth about moral reality and was corroborated statistically by scientists such as Edward Green, senior research scientist at Harvard's School of Public Health and director of its AIDS Prevention Research Project. Yet more than four thousand press releases said the Pope was ignorant. A former French prime minister, Alain Juppé, speaking as though from a high moral platform, said, "This Pope is beginning to pose a problem" and "is living in a situation of total autism."[23]

The Sanhedrin said much of the same of Christ. But Christ, who is the Beginning, is also the End, and so He always has the last word. He speaks to the Pharisees of all ages: "If you were blind, you would have no sin; but now you are saying 'We see,' so your sin remains" (John 9:41).

March 29, 2009

---

[23] "France Condemns Pope's Remarks on Condoms in Africa," Reuters, March 18, 2009, http://www.reuters.com/.

ALLEGORY

In *As You Like It*, Shakespeare spoke of all the world as a stage. He invoked the stage to represent human experience, just as William Jennings Bryan spoke of a "cross of gold" to stand for his day's controversial gold standard. Bryan may have been something of a blowhard, and certainly not Shakespeare's aesthetic twin, but both mastered the art of metaphor—using a word as a stand-in for something else. If you stretch out a metaphor, you get an allegory, so that a narrative poem such as Virgil's *Aeneid* represents all the ups and downs of life, and Tolkien's *Lord of the Rings* is palpably about Christian spiritual combat, even though Tolkien strongly denied that his Catholicism infused it.

It is tempting to embrace Holy Week as the greatest of all allegories—"the greatest story ever told"—for the tragedy and triumph of Christ do indeed surpass all other stories. The flaw and danger is that such rhetoric might give the impression that it is only a story, loose with facts and too emotive to have actually happened. The apostles did not think so. They were so shocked by it that the risen Christ had to coax them out of their moral stupor and show them that He was not a ghost, just as He berated the two men on the Emmaus road for not having understood that these events had to happen.

In long retrospect, the days from Palm Sunday to Easter were not an allegory; more precisely, they were what every noble allegory tries to portray. Man is the allegory and Christ is the fact, and the whole life of grace consists in growing day by day into that fact, rather than living as half human, compromised by sin, like a machine with a dying battery.

The life of Christ is not an allegory; our lives are an allegory of the life of Christ. "You have not chosen me: I have chosen you" (John 15:16).

Plato's allegory of the cave is a strong image of how we perceive existence from a limited human perspective. People chained in a cave see images illuminated by a fire behind them only as shadows cast onto the wall they face. That is the way the human intelligence perceives reality unaided by God. Christ abolishes the shadows and lets us see the ultimate realities directly: Death, Judgment, Heaven and Hell. St. Paul called our daily concerns and perceptions "things which are a mere shadow of what is to come; but the substance belongs to Christ" (Col. 2:17).

Jesus does not want those He loves to live limited lives. The old lament was, "Man is like a mere breath; his days are like a passing shadow" (Ps. 144:4). In Holy Week, the Cross is not a fabricated metaphor. It is the truth that can make our lives eternal.

March 20, 2016

The Gate of Mercy

On Palm Sunday, Our Lord entered the city that symbolizes all civilization. Jerusalem was never the same again, nor was the world. The Golden Gate through which Our Lord entered, called the Gate of Mercy (*Sha-ar Harachamin*) by the Jews, was to be the portal through which the Messiah entered history.

Refusing to believe that Jesus was the Messiah, and to thwart any Messiah's entrance in the future, the Ottoman Sultan Suleiman I blocked up the Golden Gate in 1541 and placed a cemetery outside it. But he had closed the barn door too late.

Christ cannot be kept out of history. He can be kept out of individual lives, though, and He can be repudiated by the civilization He shaped. Many who despise the Christian civilization of which they are part refuse to acknowledge that without the Holy Spirit, those attributes of civilization they enjoy, and even exploit, cannot be sustained.

George Weigel recently pointed out that without the cohesive vision of man revealed in Christ there would be no concept of the freedom and of the dignity of man—which logically led to the dignity of woman, the abolition of slavery, freedom of expression, and the sanctity of life in all its stages. Nor would there be knowledge of creation, rational order, or a purpose for history—which is the matrix for physical science and the university.

Without Christ, the plastic and musical arts would not have attained their highest achievements, nor would there even be humor in its most benign and self-satirical forms—for that is based on humility, which is not a developed virtue outside the Judeo-Christian tradition. The noblest pagans had no concept of humility.

Cultural progress is not inevitable, and it is possible to regress to a barbaric state. Theocratic legal systems that do not recognize Christian justice as we know it allow rights for nonbelievers only as a privilege that can be withdrawn. We need only look back on the Marxist and National Socialist empires to see the consequences of blocking the gates of civilization to the Messiah. Barbarians always are milling about, and civilization admits them to its own peril.

In Holy Week, Our Lord reminds us that if the voices of the prophets and saints are silenced, the very stones of civilization will cry out in His praise (Luke 19:40). The human will has the choice to welcome its Messiah or to fall silent, but in that silence can be heard a terrible destruction at work. The Church opens her heart to the Lord in Holy Week and resumes annually the joyful task of transforming civilization, and that can be accomplished in the city only when it is accomplished in individual souls.

"Lift up your heads, O ye gates, and be ye lift up, ye everlasting doors; and the King of glory shall come in" (Psalm 24:7).

March 16, 2008

FAITHFUL THOMAS

The greatest week of the year introduces the Triduum—the glorious three days that have changed the world forever—as a procession. All life is a procession in the obvious movement from yesterday to today to tomorrow. The physical procession walked on Palm Sunday begins the steps we walk daily with Our Lord to His temporary tomb. None of this is "play-acting" like a Passion Play; while still in time, we actually are with Our Lord.

In recent years, there has been a widespread loss of the numinous character of the Liturgy whereby heaven and earth meet. The less a people understand the true drama of the authentic rites, the more they lapse into tasteless theatrics and contrived sentimentality, rather like the old vaudevillians who wrapped themselves in a flag or held a baby when their act was failing. Happily, the Church in many places is beginning to recover from the unfortunate generation of abuses in worship. Step by step, younger people are being introduced to their great heritage in the solemn chants and actions of the sacred rites. In addition, there are nonliturgical devotions to help the faithful, such as the Stations of the Cross. This year, for the first time in a long while, the Liturgy of the Passion on Good Friday will be preceded in the Church of St. Michael by the Three Hours Devotion from noon to three, with meditations on the Seven Last Words.

Walking with Our Lord in these days requires faith and reason. In his 1998 encyclical *Fides et Ratio*, Pope John Paul II wrote: "Faith and reason are like two wings on which the human spirit rises to the contemplation of truth; and God has placed in the human heart a desire to know the truth — in a word, to know himself — so that, by knowing and loving God, men and women may also come to the fullness of truth about themselves (cf. Exod. 33:18; Ps. 27:8–9; 63:2–3; John 14:8; 1 John 3:2)."

A prime example of this is the apostle Thomas. His ardor was seen when he was willing to risk his life by going with Christ to Jerusalem (see John 11:16). These were not empty words: tradition has him traveling to Syria and Persia and dying for his Lord in India. But his faith also exercised his reason. He asks the Lord where He is going, because he does not know (John 14:5). After the Resurrection, he says he will not believe that it is the Lord unless he can touch the wounds (John 20:25).

These are examples of doubt, but a doubt that is reasonable. Our Lord obliges by declaring Himself "The Way, the Truth and the Life" (John 14:6). And on the eighth day of the Resurrection, He moves Thomas to utter what Pope Benedict XVI called the greatest profession of faith in the Scriptures: "My Lord and my God!" (John 20:28).

In these great days, let us walk with the whole Church, including that apostle called Doubting Thomas, who in fact was Rational Thomas and Faithful Thomas.

April 13, 2014

Salvation from the Ultimate Slavery

We cannot overestimate the gift of the Resurrection, which frees mortal humanity from eternal death. This is the ultimate freedom. All other desires to be free in one form or another, which are the natural urgings of man to realize his dignity, are metaphors for freedom from death.

During Lent, the civil calendar marked the two hundredth anniversary of the abolition of slavery in the British Empire, which would be prelude, a couple of generations later, to abolition in our country. The crucial figure in that movement was William Wilberforce, about whom an excellent film is now being shown. It touches on, but not enough, I think, the Christian inspiration for his endeavors. He was an evangelically inclined member of the Established Church of England. Of his four sons, three became Catholic, and important figures in the Oxford movement. I was privileged to know his great-grandson, a devout Catholic gentleman.

Slavery took many forms throughout history and is wrongly understood simply as a racial phenomenon. In most forms of slavery over the ages, people were enthralled by members of their own race, and in many times slaves were important educators and had political influence. Slavery in all its forms degrades the enslaver by its assumption that one of God's children has a right to "own" another of God's children.

Where Christianity was disdained, slavery flourished. Many people also defended slavery in the name of a twisted concept of Christianity. The abolition of slavery was a Christian achievement, and where slavery remains in the world today, it is promoted by enemies of Christianity.

The great St. Anselm, an archbishop of Canterbury who was born of Burgundian parents in Tuscany, held a church council in London in 1102 that abolished slavery in no uncertain terms. "Let no one hereafter presume to engage in that nefarious trade in which hitherto in England men were usually sold like brute animals."[24] Offenders of this abolitionist decree were subject to excommunication.

The mysterious and — for the lukewarm — unpleasant reality is that if we allow ourselves to be enslaved to mortal sin by the Prince of Lies, we are excommunicated for all eternity, and the word for that is damnation. In the first Eucharistic Prayer, we pray to be saved from this damnation. Christ saves us from that.

Our parish is dedicated to Our Savior, and churches are not dedicated to platitudes. We need salvation. To be enslaved to sin is worse than to be enslaved to some ancient Persian overlord or a more modern Simon Legree. On Palm Sunday, Our Savior entered the Golden Gate of Jerusalem to break the chains of death and abolish eternal slavery. This is the world's greatest joy, and in these holy days, all the solemn ceremonies, by their very solemnity, celebrate the intensity of that immeasurable triumph that Christ won by His own blood.

April 1, 2007

---

[24] "Slavery, III (History of)," *New Catholic Encyclopedia, Encyclopedia.com*, accessed May 19, 2017, http://www.encyclopedia.com/.

THE ONE DRAMA THAT IS REAL

W hen Philip brought some Greeks to Christ, Our Lord said, almost as a hymn: "The hour has come for the Son of Man to be glorified" (John 12:23). This happened after He had entered Jerusalem in an extravagant fashion: He who often fled from crowds orchestrated a triumphant pageant to fit what the prophets had said about how the Messiah would enter the holy city. He may also have sardonically been conforming to the protocols of majesty to embarrass the pompous authorities, who gave undue importance to appearances.

We know little about Philip after the Resurrection, save for an uncertain tradition that he preached in Phrygia and was martyred at Hierapolis. That we know little about him says much about him: his whole function was to become invisible so that people might see Jesus through him. This is a definition of sanctity: *cupio dissolvi*—to disappear so that Christ might appear (Phil. 1:23). Philip's lack of self-consciousness helped him first to introduce Nathanael to Christ (John 1:45); then he brought crowds.

In Philip, we see what Archbishop Fénelon tried to describe to the future king of France and to many others tempted with gossamer glory: "God's glory so expands itself, and so fills the mind, that the other motive, that of our own happiness, becomes so small, and so recedes from our inward notice, as to be practically annihilated. It is then that God becomes what he ever ought to be—the center of the soul, to which all its affections tend; the great moral sun of the soul, from which all its light and all its warmth proceed."[25]

[25] François Fénelon, *Maxims of the Saints*, art. 2.

In Holy Week, the Liturgies are not a performance that we watch. We are on the stage, and the stage is not a theater but the world itself. This is the one drama among all dramas that is real, for it is the entire experience of the human race, all that was and will be, encapsulated in a few days. Christ "recapitulates" the encounter of man and God in Himself. As Pope Benedict says, Jesus is "the face of God," and in these days that face is broken and bleeding as proof that God, who made the drama, is also in the drama.

In Holy Week, the Christian should be like Philip when he brought foreigners to Christ. There are many in our city who say, like those Greek visitors, "Sir, we would see Jesus" (John 12:21). The merely curious sightseers in our city say that, as do those earnestly seeking baptism, for they are reaching for Christ the Way. The cynics in our city say that because their disdain for humbug is a fugitive desire for Christ the Truth. The atheists in our city say that, for every deadening denial of the existence of Christ is their gasping for Christ the Life.

April 5, 2009

GREATNESS AND GOODNESS

It seems to me that greatness exists on two levels. One is that of those who do important things for the general society. Historians may debate whether this encompasses bad as well as good things. After all, there have been figures in history who were called great because they affected the world importantly, if dolorously. Napoleon changed the world in many ways, but he did so cruelly, at the cost of hundreds of thousands of lives and the exaction of unimaginable suffering. Then there have been those who saved civilization from near calamity.

If greatness as moral good is not part of the calculus, then bad men as well as good can be called great, if their influence was vast, and whether for the good or for the bad. Stalin and Mao Tse-tung, for instance, killed more people and imposed more horrors than anyone else in history, but through the lens of moral indifference, they were great figures, if only because their crimes were on such a scale.

From a moral perspective, greatness is the peculiar laurel of those who have not done things on a great scale, but who did things that were good in defiance of things bad. As a teenager, I had already decided that Winston Churchill was a great man for the good, so in 1961 I persuaded my father—the greatest of men in my life—to accompany me into Manhattan to see Churchill when he visited Bernard Baruch. There was no conversation, only a nod and pleasing comment. It was all I needed for contact with greatness.

Later I read that Churchill thought the three most regrettable sadnesses were those of lives worn down by toil, worry, and boredom. For all his hard work and worries and boring years as a man scorned, Churchill was never worn down by them. That is a matter of natural virtue and a key to moral greatness. Yet Jesus was more than a great man that way. When He entered Jerusalem on Palm Sunday, some — guileless children and wizened elders — cheered Him as a great man, but He was more than that, and anyone who defines Him as only that misses the point. His divine nature, perfectly united with His human nature, exulted in common carpentry, just as much as He did in summoning all the galaxies into existence from the first light. His human worries were a descant on His insight into how heavy human hearts missed the fugitive beauty of the lilies of the field. Nothing bored Him: not a single sparrow, nor a hair on a head.

On the first Palm Sunday, those who remained with Jesus were transformed: work would be a votive offering and not a burden; worry would gentle into prudence; and boredom would be banished. For proof, there is the fact that Jesus the toiler would not worry about what the Father had prepared. And He who never was bored was the only man who never bored anyone.

March 29, 2015

A Loftier Judgment

As Christ moved day by day toward the Cross, the Palm Sunday crowds thinned out. So it is in every generation when the Holy Church takes stands inhospitable to the regnant conceits of the age. There were no fair-weather friends on Calvary. By tracing Our Savior's footsteps in this Holy Week, we sign up with Him and against His foes. Some crucified Him out of ignorance and others out of malice, but the motives did not mitigate the suffering.

Since the Passion was the mystery of God's love beyond human comprehension, Jesus said from the Cross that even those who acted viciously for their own ends did not know what they were doing. And there were those who, like the daydreams of Adam, would try to make themselves God, in an exercise of what Newman called "those giants, the passion and pride of man."[26]

Christ was crucified by some who invoked religion to justify themselves. It was not like the politician who recently said she was praying to St. Joseph to pass a health-care bill that the Catholic bishops have said violates the sanctity of life and the freedom of conscience. That legislation is the most recent reminder that the Passion of Christ, victorious once and for all, is nonetheless relived in every spiritual struggle. This is why Pascal said that Christ is in agony until the end of the world. He said that because Christ Himself said: "I tell you the truth, whatever you did for one of the least of these brothers of mine, you did for me" (Matt. 25:40).

---

[26] Newman, *The Idea of a University*, discourse 5, section 9.

Pontius Pilate and Herod struck a deal so that Christ might die. By their compromise, they "became friends with each other that very day" (Luke 23:12). Christ did not bring them together; their rejection of Christ did. Any legislation that denies constitutional rights will be subject to judicial review, and the present health bill, which will impose an estimated half a trillion dollars in new taxes, will be answerable in the next election, but any legislation that achieves its ends by canceling Christ out of the social equation will be answerable to a loftier judgment. Pilot and Herod claimed they were acting for the good of the people. Pilate seems to have acted out of a lack of wisdom, and Herod out of a lack of intelligence. The compromise they reached was the alchemy of disaster. Likewise, those in our day who think that the promise of an executive order will prevent taxpayer funding of abortion are sadly mistaken. They may think they have secured "peace for our time," and may even say to their friends, as Chamberlain told the British people in 1938: "And now I recommend you to go home and sleep quietly in your beds." And, whether naïve or dense, they will give thanks that Poland was never invaded, and unborn life is safe.

March 28, 2010

CHRIST ENTERS THE CITY

This Lent has seen in play the adage—almost a law—that the amount of time required to complete a task is equal to the amount of time available. Last year, Easter was almost as early as it can ever be, and all was accomplished on time. This year, Easter is almost as late as it can ever be, and there still is a bit of a rush to get ready. But every year the Lord is in charge, while He entrusts His creation to human creatures as His cooperators in making the world anew.

By the Incarnation, Christ, who is the "Word made Flesh," led mankind, as true man, to divine glory, as true God. "God did not appoint angels to be rulers of the world to come, and that world is what we are talking about.... As it was his purpose to bring a great many of his sons into glory, it was appropriate that God, for whom everything exists and through whom everything exists, should make perfect, through suffering, the leader who would take them to their salvation" (Heb. 2:5, 10).

When the Savior announced that He would go to Jerusalem to "awaken" His friend Lazarus, Thomas volunteered himself and his fellow apostles to accompany Jesus on what they thought was a suicide mission: "Let us also go, that we may die with Him" (John 11:16). When Jesus came to the outskirts of Bethany, He was met by St. Martha, who on an earlier occasion had kept to herself in the kitchen: "Lord, if you had been here, my brother would not have died" (John 11:21). In each instance is seen the transforming power of Christ's love, a potency over human hearts that would come into full play in the Passion.

Today Jesus enters Manhattan as once He entered Jerusalem, and the characters in the city are the same, for cities may change, but human nature does not. Whether He enters by the Royal Gates or the Brooklyn Bridge, the avenues have their cheering crowds, sullen bystanders, cynics, traitors, and worshippers. The mass media may try to make sense of it, or ignore it, but the procession goes on, with its innocent children, anxious apostles, and curious onlookers: "If these were silent, the very stones would cry out" (Luke 19:40).

There, too, with an air of condescension and irritation, are the governors and judges and savants who resent this intrusion into their establishment. As Christ enters the city, He judges every personality, and this He does simply by a glance of His eye and the look on His face: His merciful presence is more wonderfully salvific and frightfully damning than any word.

> Rise up, LORD, let men not be complacent:
>> Let the nations come before you to be judged.
> Put fear into them, LORD:
>> Let them know that they are only men.
> (Ps. 9:19–20)

April 17, 2011

THE FLESH AND BLOOD OF THIS JESUS

In the holiest week of the year, Lent ends with the Wednesday liturgies. The Triduum begins with Holy Thursday, commemorating the institution of the Sacred Priesthood and Eucharist. Christ provides this heavenly food for our brief earthly lifetime of service to Him. Holy Thursday renews the adoration of Christ's Presence at the altar. Our world has forgotten the Mass to a shocking and, literally, deadly degree. The soul starves without the Mass.

Failure to adore Christ in the Mass comes from the curse of self-adoration. This is as old as the human race. In our day it has been furthered by wrong teaching about the Eucharist. Seven years ago, the Church formed a Vox Clara (clear voice) commission to provide a more accurate translation of the sacred texts as well as encourage use of the sonorous Latinity that is the universal heritage of the Western Rite. Many have been working on this, and I was assigned a small part in it, from which experience I have learned how difficult it is to translate authentically.

Much of the Novus Ordo (revised Mass) has not been satisfactory, and to this problem have been added many abuses that the Holy See is now also attempting to reform. In this holy season, new instructions and admonitions will be published. Some liturgists who already protest that it will be hard to adjust to this are the same people who promoted changes so radical that they have been devastating to Eucharistic worship. Their "renewal" has resulted in a 50 percent decline in Mass attendance in the past generation and a growing ignorance of the Real Presence.

We do not change the Mass. The Mass changes us. St. Gregory of Nyssa said that the Blessed Sacrament of Christ's Body and Blood is not so much consumed by us as we are consumed by it. In recent years, our society has suffered substance abuse, sexual abuse, financial abuse, marriage abuse, and countless offenses against the natural order. The most devastating abuse is to abuse Christ. To abuse the Mass is to crucify Christ and to "eat and drink to our own condemnation." The two go together, for as St. John Chrysostom says, in the Eucharist "we become a single body ... members of His flesh and bone of His bone.... He blends Himself with us so that we might become one single entity."[27]

In second-century Rome, St. Justin Martyr, who was beheaded under Marcus Aurelius, told the emperor: "We come together to celebrate the Eucharist. No one is allowed to partake except those who believe as true the things which we teach.... We do not receive this food as ordinary bread and as ordinary drink. We are taught that the food over which the prayer of thanksgiving, the word received from Christ, has been said ... is the flesh and blood of this Jesus who became flesh."[28]

April 4, 2004

---

[27] St. John Chrysostom, *Homily on John* 46.3.
[28] St. Justin Martyr, *First Apology* 66.

EASTERTIDE

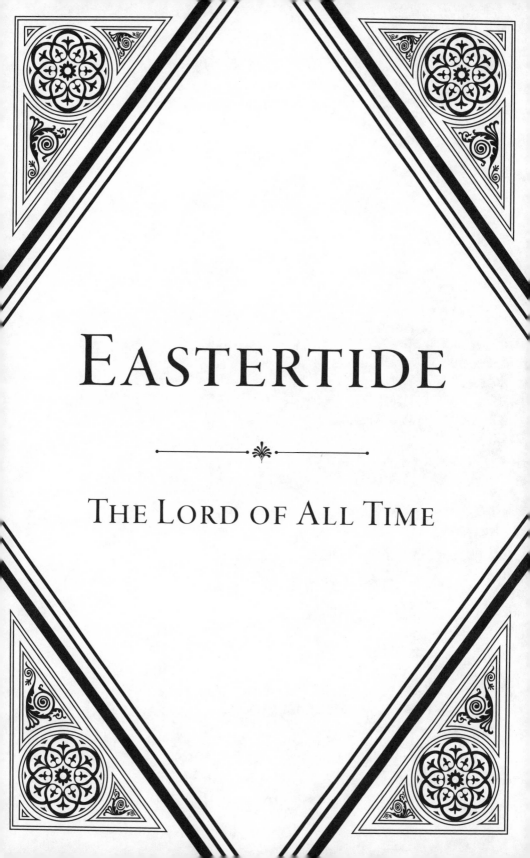

THE LORD OF ALL TIME

You, O Death, Are Annihilated

This week, in place of the regular pastor's column, we share the Paschal joy of the Hieratikon (Catechetical Sermon) of Saint John Chrysostom (ca. 347–407), archbishop of Constantinople and Doctor of the Church. Because of his inspired eloquence, he was given the nickname ὁ Χρυσόστομος — or, in our modern alphabet "chrysostomos" — meaning "golden mouthed." As he is the patron saint of preachers, his icon hangs directly above the pulpit in our church.

EASTER SERMON OF ST. JOHN CHRYSOSTOM
BISHOP OF CONSTANTINOPLE (CA. 400)

Are there any who are devout lovers of God?
    Let them enjoy this beautiful bright festival!
    Are there any who are grateful servants?
    Let them rejoice and enter into the joy of their Lord!
    Are there any weary with fasting?
    Let them now receive their wages!

If any have toiled from the first hour, let them receive their due reward;

If any have come after the third hour, let him with gratitude join in the Feast!

And he that arrived after the sixth hour, let him not doubt; for he too shall sustain no loss. And if any delayed until the ninth hour, let him not hesitate; but let him come too.

And he who arrived only at the eleventh hour, let him not be afraid by reason of his delay. For the Lord is gracious and receives the last even as the first. He gives rest to him that comes at the eleventh hour, as well as to him that toiled from the first.

To this one He gives, and upon another He bestows; He accepts the works as He greets the endeavor. The deed He honors and the intention He commends.

Let us all enter into the joy of the Lord!

First and last alike receive your reward; rich and poor, rejoice together!

Sober and slothful, celebrate the day! You that have kept the fast, and you that have not, rejoice today for the Table is richly laden! Feast royally on it; the calf is a fatted one. Let no one go away hungry.

Partake, all, of the cup of faith. Enjoy all the riches of His goodness!

Let no one grieve at his poverty, for the universal kingdom has been revealed.

Let no one mourn that he has fallen again and again; for forgiveness has risen from the grave. Let no one fear death, for the Death of Our Savior has set us free.

He has destroyed it by enduring it. He destroyed Hell when He descended into it. He put it into an uproar even as it tasted of His flesh.

Isaiah foretold this when he said,

"You, O Hell, have been troubled by encountering Him below."

Hell was in an uproar because it was done away with. It was in an uproar because it is mocked. It was in an uproar, for it is destroyed. It is in an uproar, for it is annihilated. It is in an uproar, for it is now made captive.

Hell took a body, and discovered God.

It took earth, and encountered Heaven.

It took what it saw, and was overcome by what it did not see.

O death, where is thy sting? O Hell, where is thy victory?

Christ is risen, and you, O death, are annihilated!

Christ is risen, and the evil ones are cast down!

Christ is risen, and the angels rejoice!

Christ is risen, and life is liberated!

Christ is risen, and the tomb is emptied of its dead; for Christ, having risen from the dead, is become the firstfruits of those who have fallen asleep.

To Him be Glory and Power forever and ever. Amen!

March 26, 2016

CHRIST IS RISEN!

The news converted thousands in Jerusalem and sent the apostles out into the world. Every parish, including ours here in Murray Hill, is the result of that most important event in history. By its uniqueness, the Resurrection elicits a response different from the normal reaction to happy news. There is doubt, of course, since it seems impossible, and when the apostles themselves heard the report from the women at the tomb, "these words seemed to them an idle tale, and they did not believe them" (Luke 24:11). And there was fear mingled because this had to do with death and another realm of existence, so that while the cynic may think something is too good to be true, the witnesses on Easter were tempted to think that this appearing of Christ might be too true to be good. The women at the tomb "departed quickly from the tomb with fear and great joy" (Matt. 28:8), and in the Upper Room the apostles "were startled and frightened, and supposed that they saw a spirit" (Luke 24:37).

But now servile fear of the unknown is changed to holy fear of the known. We have been blessed with unprecedented numbers of worshippers who have shown true devotion, and orderly patience, too, at times when they had to wait on the street for a while before entering the church. I certainly am thankful that Providence provided some visiting priests, and those priests did heroic work in hearing so many confessions for so many hours.

As we continue to live in the glory of the Resurrection, we pray for Pope Benedict XVI, who will be coming to our city in this Easter season. In his homily at the Easter Vigil in Rome, he said:

In the early Church there was a custom whereby the Bishop or the priest, after the homily, would cry out to the faithful: "Conversi ad Dominum"—"Turn now towards the Lord." This meant in the first place that they would turn towards the East, towards the rising sun, the sign of Christ returning, whom we go to meet when we celebrate the Eucharist. Where this was not possible, for some reason, they would at least turn towards the image of Christ in the apse, or towards the Cross, so as to orient themselves inwardly towards the Lord. Fundamentally, this involved an interior event; conversion, the turning of our soul towards Jesus Christ and thus towards the living God, towards the true light. Linked with this, then, was the other exclamation that still today, before the Eucharistic Prayer, is addressed to the community of the faithful: *Sursum corda*—"Lift up your hearts," high above the tangled web of our concerns, desires, anxieties and thoughtlessness—"Lift up your hearts, your inner selves!" In both exclamations we are summoned, as it were, to a renewal of our Baptism: Conversi ad Dominum—we must distance ourselves ever anew from taking false paths, onto which we stray so often in our thoughts and actions. We must turn ever anew towards him who is the Way, the Truth and the Life. We must be converted ever anew, turning with our whole life towards the Lord. And ever anew we must allow our hearts to be withdrawn from the force of gravity, which pulls them down, and inwardly we must raise them high: in truth and love.

At this hour, let us thank the Lord, because through the power of his word and of the holy Sacraments, he points us in the right direction and draws our heart upwards. Let us pray to him in these words: "Yes, Lord, make us Easter people, men and women of light, filled with the fire of your love. Amen."[29]

March 30, 2008

[29] Benedict XVI, Homily, March 22, 2008.

THE SUBLIME WAYFARER

In all the accounts of the Resurrection, there is surprise. If it had been expected, future generations might have said it was a hallucination. There was also confusion about Christ's risen body: its ability to materialize in a room with locked doors and maintain its completely natural appearance while obscuring its identity. These were traits without precedent in human experience.

On the road to Emmaus, those two men took for granted the figure that started to walk along with them, and even expressed a certain irritation at what seemed to be the Man's ignorance of what had happened on Friday. Looking back, we can see this as a form of prayer. The two disciples were in conversation with the Lord, confiding in Him their concerns and wondering at the same time if He was "on their wavelength." If prayer is real, it will not be a stilted conversation, like something read by rote from the back of a prayer card, however helpful such words may be as promptings. God is much more patient with us than we are with Him.

On the Emmaus road, the Lord calmly explains why things had to be the way they were, and in this He shows the teaching office of the Church. Still unaware of the Man's identity, the disciples are nonetheless moved by His words and His presence, rather like thoughtful agnostics. So they beg Him to stay with them. In the wayside inn, He mysteriously becomes recognizable "in the breaking of the bread" (Luke 24:30–31). This is the Eucharistic revelation sung in the *Mysterium Fidei* of the Liturgy: "Christ has died. Christ is risen. Christ will come again." The Eucharist is a sacred meal, for it is Bread from Heaven, but the wounds that Christ retains on His risen body signal that this is also the sacrifice of Christ to the Father, a singular and perfect sacrifice that cannot be repeated, but that we share in by its timelessness.

In 2004, St. John Paul II wrote: "Amid our questions and difficulties, and even our bitter disappointments, the divine Wayfarer continues to walk at our side, opening to us the Scriptures and leading us to a deeper understanding of the mysteries of God."[30] When that Wayfarer vanishes, the two men rush out to tell others what has happened. This is the "Go forth" moment of the Mass, when the priest tells the people, "*Ite missa est*" — you are sent.

If there is no urgency to tell others about Christ, then His Body — the Church — is misunderstood as an institution kept alive by bureaucrats who act as embalmers, cynically sustaining a corporate identity with mendacity and mummery. That is a formula for spiritual burnout. Such burnout is the malady of people who never were on fire to begin with. But those who encounter Christ say daily: "Did not our hearts burn within us ...?" (Luke 24:32).

May 4, 2014

---

[30] John Paul II, Apostolic Letter *Mane Nobiscum Domine*, October 7, 2004, no. 2.

TRANSFORMATION

The liturgies of the first week of Easter speak of "this Easter Day," since the power of the Resurrection is not confined to the first twenty-four hours but rather melts all the days of the octave into one whole. The rest of the forty days belongs to "this Easter Season." Forty days seem to be the length of chronological time the Risen Lord spent with the apostles and others, laying the groundwork for the Church. On one occasion He appeared to more than five hundred, most of whom were still living when St. Paul wrote his first letter to the Corinthians. The tremendous impact of those encounters made the rapid spread of the gospel throughout the known world something unique in history.

When we speak of history, we must remember that a scientific categorization of human events, as opposed to oral traditions and literary epics, was in an early stage of development. The Acts (in Greek, *praxeis*) of the Apostles is one of the first writings that we would recognize as what we call a historical record, replete with psychological portraits of personalities. But both the Roman Tacitus and the Jewish Josephus, as historians, note the phenomenon of the followers of Jesus willingly dying for the Master, when they were free to renounce Him and save their own necks. A most palpable proof of the power of Easter is the way it transformed lives. These people were radically changed and then changed others. St. Paul writes singularly beautiful words to explain his own conversion. The transformation of St. Peter ranks first in importance because it was he on whom Christ established the "line of command" in the Church.

As with Paul, Peter dramatically denied Our Lord before his total conversion, and surely this was of a divine design, so that we might see the Resurrection power as a radical impact and not just the gradual intensification of a point of view. Peter denied Christ three times. Then, after the Resurrection, Christ elicited from him a threefold affirmation of love and then sent him off eventually to Rome. That was a long way from the fishing village of Capernaum. And likewise, Peter's majestic speech in Jerusalem on Pentecost demonstrated an astonishing change in this man whose natural rhetoric was halting and rough.

When Peter hung upside down on a cross in Rome, it was not therapy. It was a sacrifice of the self as joyful as it was painful, in the hope of Resurrection. Not a vain hope, for it was the confidence of the first man to have seen Christ's grave cloths lying neatly rolled up in the empty tomb. As Cardinal Newman wrote, "No one will die for his own calculations; he dies for realities."[31]

April 15, 2007

---

[31] John Henry Newman, *An Essay in Aid of a Grammar of Assent*, 1, 4, 3.

Meet Him in the Blessed Sacrament

Jesus of Nazareth was killed, and then He killed death. This is why the Church exists. Jesus planned the Church during three years of preaching, provided the Eucharist in the Upper Room, fought Satan on the Cross, reappeared on the third day, gave the apostles power to forgive sins, spent forty days teaching, and then mysteriously entered eternity. The Holy Spirit entered the apostles and got the Church going on Pentecost.

I apologize for this crude reporting of the events, but they are breathtaking. Jesus knows our limitations, so He helps us in sensory ways. He leaves His shroud lying by the tomb. He walks with the men on the Emmaus road and shows a sense of humor about their perplexity and self-absorption. Then He takes them to a "wayside inn" (an elegant way of describing the equivalent of a modern highway rest stop) and gives them food. Always food. He knows that even His own apostles with their limited mentality would find it easier to call Him a ghost than the real thing, so He eats food in front of them.

The apostles never had to "prove" that Jesus rose from the dead. They had seen Him. Later, Paul will refer nonchalantly to the witnesses still alive in his audience. I do not have to prove to you that the World Trade Center was horribly destroyed in a couple of hours. I take for granted that you know that. So it is, but in a jubilant way, with the Resurrection of Christ.

In the next few weeks I hope to give some bits of information about the Resurrection. This is called *catechesis*, which is a Greek word for "teaching." In theology, facts sound more impressive when you use Greek words, just as menus are more impressive—and expensive—when you use French words.

In this Easter season, stop by the church and light a candle before the Risen Christ in the Blessed Sacrament. Since the first Easter, you can meet Him in the Blessed Sacrament in any church. That is a practical result of the Resurrection. I have found Him there all the way from Sydney to San Francisco. In Jerusalem, I had a feeling that He was asking me why I had spent that time and money, when He was back in Manhattan.

You might also want to see *The Lord of the Rings* film. Few critics mention that it is an allegory of the Resurrection. The author, J.R.R. Tolkien, was a wonderful Catholic, whose mother sacrificed much for the Faith. He used to attend Mass daily in a church where I was a priest.

March 31, 2002

Joy Is a Fact

The joy of Easter is more than happiness, since happiness is a feeling, whereas joy is a fact. Happiness comes from impressions, whereas joy comes from comprehension. Happiness with what is bad quickly turns to sadness. Joy is being happy with what is good. As only God is good (Luke 18:19), endless joy comes from encounter with Him who is eternal: "So also you now indeed have sorrow; but I will see you again, and your heart shall rejoice; and your joy no man shall take from you" (John 16:22).

That blessed happiness toward which all human activity tends needs knowledge of truth to become the "fullness of joy" that Jesus promised (John 15:11). When the Risen Christ appeared, no one laughed. The witnesses were "afraid, yet filled with joy" (Matt. 28:8). It was too joyful to be a laughing matter. This is why the Church's most joyful liturgies are "solemn." To reduce worship of the Risen Christ to a merely human party would be like turning the Heavenly City into a suburb.

Because Easter is direct contact with things eternal, we have to work at understanding its joy, and at first it may not seem "joyful" at all. It is easier to relate to the happiness of Christmas and the sorrow of Good Friday, since all of us were born and will die. But only when they are perceived as marking the birth and death of the Son of God do these occasions become joyful. The Resurrection permits no sentimentalizing, unless it is turned into a festival of spring and vague immortality, but that evaporates quickly, and even the flowers and birds do not pay tribute south of the equator.

Jesus told Peter: "What I am doing you do not understand now; but afterward you will understand" (John 13:7). Just before his own crucifixion, around the year 64, when Rome was in flames, Peter described the Risen Christ "in whom also now, though you see Him not, you believe; and believing shall rejoice with joy unspeakable and glorified" (1 Peter 1:8).

This Holy Week, our parish attracted the largest throngs I can remember, people often standing outside on Park Avenue, unable to get in. In part, I think it was a response to the unprofessional and even hysterical calumnies of some journalists against St. Peter's successor, Benedict XVI. Mostly it was a response to Christ among us. The Pope said on Easter: "Joy cannot be commanded. It can only be given. The Risen Lord gives us joy: true life. We are already held forever in the love of the One to whom all power in heaven and on earth has been given."[32]

April 11, 2010

---

[32] Benedict XVI, Homily, April 3, 2010.

"Gold and Silver Have I None"

The rare honor of a papal visit to our nation, and specifically to our city, comes most happily in the time of Easter. Pope Benedict XVI is the 264th successor of St. Peter, whose preaching converted three thousand in Jerusalem on Pentecost. Our present Holy Father will preach the same Gospel as Peter in various ways in different places, rejoicing in the modern means of communication that will carry his message to many millions beyond those who physically will be in his presence. The Pope will be among us in New York on Friday, Saturday, and Sunday, April 18–20, having traveled here from Washington, D.C.

In preparation, the people of the archdiocese have been praying that many who hear the Pope will be converted to belief in the Risen Christ, that those who have grown lukewarm will be quickened in their faith, that the lapsed will return to the sacraments, that other Christians will be reunited to the One Fold of the One Shepherd, and that all believers will grow in zeal for the increase of the Catholic, Apostolic, and Roman Church.

To this end, it is urged that special visits be made to the Blessed Sacrament, and that confessions and Communions be offered for the Pope's intentions. On this Third Sunday of Easter, we are bid to pray especially that as we celebrate the bicentennial year of the archdiocese, we may, like the Emmaus disciples, recognize Jesus in the breaking of the bread, and carry out our mission to make him known to others. On April 13, the Fourth Sunday of Easter, the special intention is that as we prepare for the Pope's arrival, we may have pride in our ancestors, and gratitude to God, for all that has been accomplished in our archdiocese in just two hundred years.

These bicentennial celebrations remind us also that our own parish next year will mark the fiftieth anniversary of the completion of our church building. The parish Restoration Fund has been able to do many repairs to the roof and fabric of the church, and we are now working on important interior repairs.

In all these works, we have to keep our priorities focused on our mission to proclaim the Gospel, especially in the heart of this great city. In the first year of Christian history, St. Peter, walking through the streets of Jerusalem, said to a lame man who expected alms: "Gold and silver have I none, but that which I do have give I to you: in the name of Jesus Christ of Nazareth, walk" (Acts 3:6).

Pope Benedict, in that Petrine succession, will be walking among us soon, declaring the same Christ. With the help of our prayers and fidelity, as in Jerusalem of old, many will be "filled with wonder and amazement."

April 6, 2008

THE WORK AHEAD OF US

The Risen Lord spent forty days structuring His Church and training His disciples for the work ahead of them. We may infer some of what He told them by what is recorded in the Gospel narratives and the apostolic letters. The Hebrew prophets had been part of the Resurrection drama, preparing the way even though they did not understand how their inspiration would be realized. Years after the Resurrection, St. Peter would write of these prophets:

"The Spirit of Christ which was in them foretold the sufferings of Christ and the glories that would come after them, and they tried to find out at what time and in what circumstances all this was to be expected. It was revealed to them that the news they brought of all the things which have now been announced to you, by those who preached to you the Good News through the Holy Spirit sent from heaven, was for you and not for themselves. Even the angels long to catch a glimpse of these things" (1 Pet. 1:11–12).

The neat symmetry of God's plan for His Church is glimpsed even in the way the Lord's burial cloths were found meticulously folded in the empty tomb. "God is in the details," and nothing is disordered in the way Christ orders events. He predicted the trials His Church would face in every age. There are those who find this so unnerving that they would ignore it.

One example is the way much of the "social media" and numerous political leaders downplay the persecution of Christians in many places today—and this also includes attempts to intimidate Christian witness in our own country. Recently, people foolishly (and some agitators by cynical calculation) were obsessed with what turned out to be false journalism about mayhem and rape in our universities. Others, from congressmen to basketball players, spent weeks waving their raised arms in empathy with a shooting incident whose reported details proved to have been false. Yet there is an embarrassed silence about Christians being crucified, beheaded, stoned, and shot in country after country.

At the papal ceremonies on Good Friday, the Holy Father's preacher, Father Raniero Cantalamessa lamented that the slaughter of Christians is taking place before "the indifference of world institutions." He compared this with the third-century martyrs during the reign of Decius and said that those who affect indifference today "risk being Pilates who wash our hands."

The motives of those who do not want to face the reality of the present persecutions may vary, and some may be more slothful than malicious. But the saints draw strength from knowing that the Lord knew all that would happen and promised joy for those who look to Him and do not look away: "The hour is coming when whoever kills you will think he is offering service to God" (John 16:2).

April 12, 2015

BEYOND ALL DESERVING

The Resurrection happened two thousand years ago. Its results are ever more alive today. The multiple tragedies and sorrows of our age can distract us from the more powerful work that Christ is doing among us. As "God is in the details," we may safely say that what the Risen Christ does in each parish is a clue to what He is doing on the world scene.

On the testimony of parishioners older than I, our parish has never witnessed such a glorious outpouring of faith as in this most recent holy season. This consecrated church was too small for the overflow that came in this Holy Week. Lines of penitents for confession extended out onto Park Avenue. If we were a vicious parish at the dawn of Good Friday, by God's grace we were a holy one by the dawn of Easter.

It is not my custom to thank people at Mass for doing their duty. We come to give thanks to God, and not to ourselves. We do not applaud our splendid choir, which volunteers many hours of time and talent. We do not applaud our staff that works overtime and our reverent altar servers. We do not applaud the ladies who volunteer to count collections and perform other tasks, or our ushers or the teachers of our CCD and RCIA and the many others. Our CCD classes for the little ones have grown so large that we need more miniature furniture. Our RCIA classes have brought many from all five continents to the Faith in this holy season. I thank them all in a subdued way, knowing that their reward will be great in Heaven.

I also thank the elderly and the infirm who make great effort to worship here, often on crutches and in wheelchairs, in ways that are physically painful. As one who has difficulty organizing himself early in the morning, I thank those mothers and fathers who *magna cum difficultate* organize their little babies to come here cheerfully. At times it is not easy to preach over the crying of babies, but such cries are the future of civilization, and God forbid that anyone be so grumpy that these distractions make one forget that all of us were crying babies ourselves once. (I exclude myself, since at the earliest stage of my infancy I was occupied with reading significant books.)

In short, God has blessed us beyond our deserving and beyond our measure. That is the gracious mercy of our Risen Lord.

If you have time, go to see the Byzantine exhibition at the Metropolitan Museum of Art. Some of the curators have been unsettled by the number of people praying before those icons. These images are a sign to us of a glory that our ancestors knew, and that in these days by God's resurrected power, we may be reliving. A blessed Easter to all of you. Christ is risen. He is risen indeed. Alleluia.

April 18, 2004

Joy That Is Not of This World

Our Lord kept his promise: "These things I have spoken to you, that my joy may be in you, and that your joy may be full" (John 15:11). Like "the peace of God, which surpasses all understanding" (Phil. 4:7), the fullness of joy transcends the ordinary experience of happiness and may not even fit the common expectation of pure happiness. The women at the empty tomb were "fearful but overjoyed" (Matt. 28:8). As the "fullness of joy" is an anticipation of Heaven, it will inevitably involve certain tension, so long as we are in time and space. To "burst with joy" or to "weep for joy" expresses the agony of ecstasy — the price paid for encountering perfection in an imperfect world. But in Heaven there is no conflict or contradiction, no exasperation at not being able to contain joy.

The culminating evidence of sanctity is a joy that is not of this world. Saints always suffer in various ways as a consequence of their heroic virtue, which pits them against the "wickedness and snares of the Devil," but there is no such thing as a sad saint. The saints are proof of the existence of God and His mercy by their very lives, which are testimonies greater even than miracles or the logic of natural theology. On Divine Mercy Sunday, the Church rejoices and publicly recognizes by infallible decree the holiness of St. John XXIII and St. John Paul II. These are the first popes to be canonized since St. Pius X, who died in 1914 and was enrolled in the calendar of saints in 1954.

Every saint is different in personality and in ways of serving the Lord, and for that reason certain ones will strike a sympathetic chord more readily than others. Some would have been easy to live with, and others decidedly difficult. But failure to rejoice in their sanctity is a judgment against us rather than against them. There is a line no less perceptive for having been mistakenly attributed to Plato: "We can easily forgive the child who is afraid of the dark, but the real tragedy is the adult who is afraid of the light." Sanctifying grace enables the light of Christ to shine not on, but through souls. "It is no longer I who live, but Christ who lives in me" (Gal. 2:20).

The Paschal candle having been lit, the joy of Easter continues, and as it does the Divine Mercy gives us new saints to help us through the valleys and hills of our days on earth. The motto of St. John XXIII was *Oboedientia et Pax* and that of St. John Paul II was *Totus Tuus*. Obedience to Christ brings peace, and if we give all we are to His Mother, we will be able to rejoice with the saints.

April 27, 2014

A MYSTERY OLD AND NEW

C. S. Lewis's book about his conversion to Christianity is called *Surprised by Joy* because he was astonished by the power of Christ to shatter his cynicism. The first Christians were very much surprised by the Resurrection, requiring Jesus to tell them to calm down. While an eager and alert mind always will be surprised by things in this world, Christians should not be surprised anymore by joy. We should expect it, while never failing to give thanks for it, because Christ is joy Himself, which the world cannot take away.

We celebrate the joy of eternal life with special solemnity in Eastertide, knowing that "solemnity" really means not dourness but elegant serenity, like a formal dance or an award ceremony. Solemnity takes us out of ourselves, and the inability to be solemn in rituals indicates self-consciousness. In this spirit, we have to give thanks to all those who selflessly have helped with the joyful solemnities of Easter. St. Paul thanked his helpers in Rome and Galatia and Corinth, and we should thank our own helpers, hoping that our parish matches the good spirit of those churches without all of their concomitant enormities.

The problem with naming names is that names inevitably are left out, because there are so many to thank. So I express a general gratitude to everyone who has been helping in this season. Of course, there are Robert Prior and our musicians, and our ushers, and the devoted women who spend many hours counting offerings, and our dutiful staff who prepare the church and help visitors. Samuel Howard and Thomas Vaniotis have been tireless in preparing our growing number of altar servers, and the liturgical results have never been finer. I do not remember so many people worshipping here. I certainly thank those many who stood for so long during the sacred rites, around the church and outside. I was not surprised by the joy of having our seminarians assist so well, and those priests who heard confessions without pause for up to six hours at a time. This was the hardest work of all and the source of much joy in Heaven.

Our Risen Lord does not make all new things. More wonderfully, he makes all things new, even things that are very old. St. Melito, bishop of the busy commercial city of Sardis in Turkey, whose birth was about as distant in time from the Resurrection as we are from the opening of the Manhattan Bridge, wrote: "The paschal mystery is at once old and new, transitory and eternal, corruptible and incorruptible, mortal and immortal. In terms of the Law it is old, in terms of the Word it is new. In its figure it is passing, in its grace it is eternal. It is corruptible in the sacrifice of the lamb, incorruptible in the eternal life of the Lord."

April 19, 2009

TO PROCLAIM THE RESURRECTION

Even in this Easter season, there are those who would nervously employ the secular convention of saying that they want Christ but not His Church, and that they can confess their sins to God without confessing to a priest. This ignores what Jesus did when He rose from the dead: He constructed the Church through His teaching during the forty days before the Ascension, and the first thing He did when He appeared to the apostles was to give them authority to forgive sins in the sacrament of reconciliation.

St. John wrote that not all the books in the world could contain what Christ did in those forty days, but the Gospel accounts tell all that He wants us to know. The power of what He taught the apostles in that brief time, with the wounds still in His body, is clear in the fact that all of them, save John himself, died brave deaths proclaiming the Resurrection.

Such dying, predicted by Christ, has perdured through all subsequent ages in one way or another. Last week, Pope Francis marked the one hundredth anniversary of the massacre of about 1.5 million Armenian Christians by the Turks, abetted by Imperial German staff officers serving with the Ottoman Empire. The Pope said that "it is necessary, and indeed a duty" to "recall the centenary of that tragic event.... Concealing or denying evil is like allowing a wound to keep bleeding without bandaging it."[33] The greatest number of killings occurred on appalling death marches of hundreds of miles where the Turks drove women, children,

---

[33] Francis, Greeting at the beginning of the Mass for the Faithful of the Armenian Rite, Vatican Basilica, April 12, 2015.

and old people (most of the young men had already been massacred) into the Syrian desert. There was no food or water given to the victims along the way—and this was done by design.

St. Paul, converted by the Risen Christ, had evangelized his homeland in Asia Minor, in a land now called Turkey. Despite centuries of persecution by Muslims, in 1914 some 15 percent of the Turkish population was Christian. Today the Christian community is practically nonexistent. Persisting in its denial of the persecution, the Turkish government condemned the honesty of Pope Francis by withdrawing its ambassador to the Holy See. That exercise in denial was not singular. In 2010, a declaration was introduced in the House of Representatives identifying the systematic eradication of the Armenians as genocide. The Obama administration blocked it.

The mentality that denies the Resurrection also denies the consequences of such denial. The Resurrection is not about spring flowers and butterflies, and Jesus made that clear by retaining the wounds in His glorified body. Christ triumphed over Satan, and to deny that is to give Satan a leg up in the governance of nations and the attitudes of people. The dominant religion of Turkey maintains that Jesus was not crucified. If not crucified, then not risen. And if not risen, then mankind has license to sink to its lowest depths by crushing life and spreading death.

April 19, 2015

ETERNAL BEAUTY

It was not enough for Professor Albert Einstein to tell the priest and physicist Father Georges Lemaître that his hypothesis of the Big Bang, which he called the "First Atomic Moment," was true. Einstein said that it was "beautiful," which was more important because its beauty located it in a symmetry larger than itself, more like music than an equation. In a deeper realm, St. Augustine said that the Gospel is a "beauty ever ancient, ever new." True beauty is ageless. This is an admonition at a time when the Easter proclamation risks becoming old news and a fading echo. St. Thomas More said that to be a real Christian is always to be surprised by the Resurrection.

Surprise permeates the primitive narratives: the groups of women as joyful as they are fearful, the two men on the Emmaus road whose hearts burn with an inexplicable astonishment, the apostles in the Upper Room stunned by what they thought might be a ghost. Had the Resurrection been exactly what they expected, there would have been no fear and no surprise.

The surprise continued when the apostle Peter preached on Pentecost by the power of the Holy Spirit and told the crowd that they could "see and hear" the results of the Resurrection (Acts 2:33). Then as now, in times ever ancient and ever new, the only alternative to that is willful blindness and deafness. This Easter, while many Christians were dying for their faith in the Resurrection in places such as Pakistan and Yemen, morally isolated people were cavorting as giant rabbits on Fifth Avenue and trampling their own children during suburban Easter egg hunts. Of the latter it may be said, "Having eyes they see not and having ears they hear not" (Ps. 115:5–6). Theirs is not the surprise of the Resurrection, but the creaking age of antique paganism.

There was a special grace at work in the death of a lady known to some of us, Mother Angelica, on Easter Day. She founded the worldwide Eternal Word Television Network starting with $200 and a garage as a studio. Our parish is fortunate that our church and rectory are used for some of its productions. While it is understandable that many were saddened that she left this world, I found it annoying that some "regretted" her "passing." There is nothing regrettable about the death of a pious woman who accomplished much for the Lord, suffered grievous physical infirmities — including two strokes — for many years, and died on the feast of the Resurrection. And as for "passing," that is what gnostic sectaries like Christian Scientists do. Faithful Christians die and do not "pass," and they pray for a happy death in the hope of eternal life.

So wrote Melito of Sardis in the second century: "The paschal mystery is at once old and new, transitory and eternal, corruptible and incorruptible, mortal and immortal. In terms of the Law it is old, in terms of the Word it is new."

April 3, 2016

Thomas Had No Doubt

Faith in the Risen Lord consists in reaction to an event, and that is why the New Testament has a book called the Acts of the Apostles and not the Thoughts of the Apostles. Some of the greatest minds ever since have thought about the Resurrection, which is why we have theology, but all that thinking has been in response to what happened. Had the Resurrection been a theory rather than a fact, no one would have been surprised by it or skeptical about the first reports of it.

Skepticism has come to mean doubt about good intentions or goodness itself, but in its classical form it meant living a simple life close to nature and not trusting authoritative statements about truth. Several centuries before the Resurrection, a Greek named Pyrrho accompanied Alexander the Great to India, where he came under the influence of philosophers who were so skeptical about reliance on material things that they did not even bother to live in houses or wear clothes.

It would be easy to classify the apostle Thomas as a skeptic, if not in the classical sense, perhaps in the modern sense of not trusting people. But "Doubting Thomas" was not doubting, so much as he was questioning. Surely Our Lord arranged for him to question the truth of what the witnesses claimed to have seen so that proof might be given. As faith is trust in a reliable source, Thomas was willing to put his faith in what the witnesses had described, but because he believed in objective truth, he wanted sensory evidence of what he had been told.

Here at work is what St. Anselm called *fides quaerens intellectum* —faith seeking understanding. Our Lord obliged Thomas by showing His wounds. Had the Resurrection been an illusion, the witnesses would have had no difficulty understanding it, because it would have been their own invention. Blessed John Henry Newman wrote: "Many persons are very sensitive of the difficulties of Religion; I am as sensitive of them as anyone; but I have never been able to see a connexion between apprehending those difficulties, however keenly, and multiplying them to any extent, and on the other hand doubting the doctrines to which they are attached. Ten thousand difficulties do not make one doubt."[34]

Our Blessed Mother had difficulty understanding how she could have a baby in her womb without the normal biological process and actually asked an angel how it could happen, but we do not call her Doubting Mary. Certainly her humility was purer than that of Thomas, but one expects that after her Son ascended in glory and sent the Holy Spirit, she and Thomas had many congenial conversations. As for Thomas, he went to India, where centuries before, Pyrrho had encountered the *gymnosophoi* skeptics, and he gave his life testifying to what he had seen and touched.

April 10, 2016

---

[34] John Henry Newman, *Apologia*, chap. 5.

"An Eye for the Times"

On this Good Shepherd Sunday, anticipating the arrival of Pope Benedict XVI to our nation and city, we are reminded that Christ the Good Shepherd has entrusted His flock to the apostles, of whom Peter is the chief and center of unity. The primacy of the Bishop of Rome, successor of Peter, is clear from the start: The angelic instruction from the Easter tomb was that the women were to tell the "disciples and Peter" (Mark 16:7), and on that same day the other apostles and those who were with them said, "The Lord has risen indeed, and has appeared to Simon!" (Luke 24:34).

St. Augustine says, "To Peter alone was it given to play the part of the whole Church.... Now it was not one man but the unity of the Church that received those keys. By this fact the preeminence of Peter was proclaimed, in that he bore the figure of the very universality and unity of the Church."

A journalist recently asked me to contribute to a symposium on what we would like to tell the Pope. I replied that it is more important that we listen to the Pope. As St. Ambrose wrote in the fourth century, "At length, Peter is set over the Church, after being tempted by the devil. And so the Lord signified beforehand what came to pass afterwards, in that He chose him to be the shepherd of the Lord's flock. For He said to him, 'When thou art converted, strengthen thy brethren'" (Luke 22:32).

We receive the Gospel in four ways—"according to" Matthew, Mark, Luke, and John. The Greek *kata* means that they record what they have received, for there is one Gospel, that of Christ Himself.

The Pope and the bishops in communion with him have the job of proclaiming and explaining that Gospel. Times and the vicissitudes of the times change, but the Church remains the means by which the sanity of the saints guides civilization through the unbalanced perceptions of mistaken theories of man. When John Henry Newman confronted social disorders in the 1850s, no less striking than that which challenges the Church today, he said in *The Idea of a University*:

> If ever there was a power on earth who had an eye for the times … such is he in the history of ages, who sits from generation to generation in the Chair of the Apostles, as the Vicar of Christ, and the Doctor of His Church. These are not the words of rhetoric, Gentlemen, but of history. All who take part with the Apostle are on the winning side…. The past never returns; the course of events, old in its texture, is ever new in its coloring and fashion. England and Ireland are not what they once were, but Rome is where it was, and St. Peter is the same.

April 13, 2008

LIVING WITH HIS LIFE
INSTEAD OF OUR OWN

This past week I remembered at the altar my maternal grandmother on what would have been her 128th birthday. Her name was Emma, just like the Queen of Hawaii who was still alive at the time of her birth, as were Ulysses S. Grant, Victor Hugo, and Cardinal Newman. It does seem long ago, but things my grandmother taught me are still fresh in my memory

Only about half that length of time separated the Resurrection of Jesus from the death of the apostle John, who remembered "that which we have heard, which we have seen with our eyes, which we have looked at and our hands have touched" (1 John 1:1).

St. Paul also writes of his encounter with the Risen Lord as though it were just yesterday, because the Resurrection was what animated him: "It is no longer I who live, but Christ who lives in me" (Gal. 2:20). This explains why he never quotes Jesus in any of his letters, nor does he refer to any of the biographical details of the Lord's life or any of His parables or miracles. All those were prelude to the all-important Resurrection.

Just as Our Lord commissioned the apostles to proclaim His triumph, so we have an urgent summons to do that today, for never has there been so much evil alive in the world, and so much ignorance about the Resurrection. The *New York Times* outdid its reputation for illiteracy about the Faith by publishing a correction: "An earlier version of this article mischaracterized the Christian holiday of Easter. It is the celebration of Jesus's resurrection from the dead, not his resurrection into heaven."[35]

On April 5, 1933, the same newspaper's Moscow correspondent, Walter Duranty, denied the deliberate starvation of millions of Ukrainians by Stalin when he wrote: "The food shortage as a whole is less grave than was believed—or, if not, at least distribution has greatly improved, which comes to the same thing for practical purposes."[36] That was the same number of years ago from us now as the Resurrection was from St. John's death.

The Holy Spirit is more accurate than the editors of the *New York Times* and has never had to publish a correction of what happened on Easter. Quite the opposite, the Sabbath was changed to Sunday in celebration, and saints ever since have broadcast what happened.

Christ died for us all so that being alive should no longer mean living with our own life, but with his life, who died for us and has risen again. And therefore, henceforward, we do not think of anybody in a merely human fashion; even if we used to think of Christ in a human fashion, we do so no longer. It follows, in fact, that when a man has become a new creature in Christ, his old life has disappeared, everything has become new about him. (2 Cor. 5:15–17).

April 14, 2013

---

[35] See Elisabetta Povoledo, "Pope Calls for 'Peace in All the World' in First Easter Message," *New York Times*, March 31, 2013; correction added on April 1, 2013, https://www.nytimes.com/.

[36] Walter Duranty, "Soviet Industry Shows Big Gains," special cable to the *New York Times*, April 6, 1933, https://www.nytimes.com/.

GENEROSITY AND THE LORD'S MERCY

There is an account of some poor man with nothing to say for himself, nonetheless begging Alexander the Great for a pittance, only to be astonished when the king handed him more than a few gold coins. "Why gold, when copper would suffice?" asked one of his officers.

The royal voice answered, "He asked as a beggar for copper coins, but I gave him as a king coins of gold." Our Lord's kingdom is not of this world, and so when men who are only of this earth ask for what would sustain them temporarily, He gives graces that will last forever.

The royal generosity of Christ is called His mercy, and it is given for a purpose. That became clear when at His bidding the apostles caught so many fish that the nets almost broke. Almost. But there never is too much for the Lord. It was something the apostles had to learn, and they never forgot it. After the Risen Lord had vanished, they even remembered that the fish numbered 153.

In the sixteenth century, the brilliant scholar and educational reformer John Colet started a school in London that provided scholarships for poor boys—admitting 153 boys each year to make the point that to obey the Lord ensures a great catch. Since then, St. Paul's School has flourished and has ornamented our culture through the hundreds of thousands of boys it has helped form into men. Just a few of them include the poet John Milton; the diarist Samuel Pepys; the war hero, first Duke of Marlborough, and ancestor of Sir Winston Churchill, John Churchill; the Revolutionary spy John André, whom George Washington regretted having to hang; the happy genius G.K. Chesterton; the testy field marshall Bernard Montgomery; and so far, three holders of the Victoria

Cross. The list goes on, in tribute to Dean Colet's confidence that God's grace would make 153 count for a lot more.

It was not irrelevant that the apostles had fished all night and caught nothing. Working hard may seem useless and discouraging, but once the voice of God is heeded, there will be a great catch. Even in the Church there are micromanagers and Dickensian clerks scratching away at their balance sheets, producing little as they ignore the voice from the shore asking with a certain heavenly whimsy, "Have you caught anything?" (John 21:5).

God's generosity is available to all who are generous enough to accept it. In the life of grace, that means opening the soul to Him. That is what confession is for. The scrupulous will doubt that we can make enough room for Him, and the presumptuous will assume that we do not have to. Recently, a kindly but ill-informed clergyman said in an interview that God's mercy is unmerited, and so there is no need to be sorry for one's sins. The fact that it is unmerited should all the more move its recipient to contrition. Alexander gave as a king, but only after the beggar begged as beggar.

April 17, 2016

The Devil Sends His Compliments

When the Church proclaims the teachings of the Risen Christ most powerfully, her antagonists pay her the compliment of getting angry, especially in the holiest season of the year. The Russian Orthodox, I am told, say that when God builds a church, Satan pitches a tent outside. In Holy Week, there were astonishing calumnies against the Pontiff himself. This is a backhanded tribute from the Prince of Lies, who knows that the Catholic Church is his one remaining obstacle to revising social reality.

After the first Easter, Peter and John were arrested for their witness to the Resurrection. As soon as they were released, these first Christians prayed: "Lord, it is you who made heaven and earth and sea, and everything in them; you it is who said through the Holy Spirit and speaking through our ancestor David, your servant: 'Why this arrogance among the nations, these futile plots among the peoples? Kings on earth setting out to war, princes making an alliance against the Lord and against his Anointed?'" (Acts 4:24–26).

Satan characteristically twists reason to rationalize, and recently he has exploited moral corruption to discredit the Church, which is the guarantor of systematic moral philosophy. When hard-pressed, the Evil One eventually reveals the hysteria behind his syllogisms. Decent journalists have been embarrassed by the bigotry and lack of professionalism in attacks by some of the media, which were encouraged in no small way by some politicians. They have exploited inexcusable moral crimes among Churchmen, which are but a very small fraction (six out of seventy-five thousand clerics last year) of similar incidents in secular organizations—from Congress and UN Peacekeeping Forces to the U.S. Swim Team and public-school educators. Credible voices now say that the Catholic Church is the safest environment for the young.

I had a pleasant exchange with Mayor Koch, in response to thanking him for his article on this topic, which was published on Holy Thursday in the *Jerusalem Post*. He wrote: "I believe the continuing attacks by the media on the Roman Catholic Church and Pope Benedict XVI have become manifestations of anti-Catholicism.... Many of those in the media who are pounding on the Church and the pope today clearly do it with delight, and some with malice. The reason, I believe, for the constant assaults is that there are many in the media, and some Catholics as well as many in the public, who object to and are incensed by positions the Church holds."[37]

While Mr. Koch does not accept all of the Church's teachings, he knows what is fair and is something like Nathaniel—the Israelite "in whom there is no guile" (John 1:47). The first apostles prayed about their foes: "And now, Lord, take note of their threats and help your servants to proclaim your message with all boldness, by stretching out your hand to heal and to work miracles and marvels through the name of your holy servant Jesus" (Acts 4:29–30).

April 18, 2010

---

[37] See "Ed Koch: Anti-Catholicism Evident in Media," Zenit, April 12, 2010, https://zenit.org/.

To Obey God Instead of Men

Our Risen Lord told Peter, "Feed my lambs. Tend my sheep. Feed my sheep" (John 21:15–17). That has been the happy burden of all Peter's successors, the popes, and of all who are baptized into Christ. The Holy Church has recently begun the process for the possible canonization of Father Emil Kapaun, a priest born in Kansas whose heroic efforts to care for the flock as a military chaplain were recognized on April 11, when he was posthumously given the Medal of Honor. The citation described his "conspicuous gallantry and intrepidity at the risk of his life above and beyond the call of duty."

Father Kapaun died in a Chinese Communist prison camp in North Korea, where he fed and nursed his starving fellow soldiers, foraging by night, finding only grass and birdseed. More than that, Father Kapaun managed to nourish his impoverished flock with the sacraments.

On the day of the Medal of Honor ceremony in the White House, the abortionist Kermit Gosnell was on trial in Philadelphia, charged on eight counts of murder, including one adult and seven newborn infants who had survived their abortions. One of his "medical" assistants had already testified to having "snipped the spines" of more than a hundred babies. The silence of most media outlets concerning this astonishing criminal case was eloquently portrayed by a photograph of the press box at the courthouse — which was nearly vacant.

Clearly, many people were made uncomfortable by the way that this case represents the logical denouement of the perverse logic of the Supreme Court's *Roe v. Wade* decision, the foundation of our Culture of Death. What happened in Gosnell's house of horrors has in fact been defended theoretically by some "ethicists" who hold positions in our universities. And many of our nation's highest officials have defended "partial-birth abortion."

The misuse of reason can rationalize contempt for life, just as happened in the Weimar Republic when the jurist Karl Binding and the psychiatrist Alfred Hoche published their defense of killing unwanted people: *Die Freigabe der Vernichtung lebensunwerten Lebens* (Allowing the destruction of life unworthy of living). Binding died in 1920, when the book was published, but Hoche lived until 1943 after privately objecting to the "euthanizing" of one of his own relatives by Nazis who had read his book and followed its principles.

As man has a free will, he is free to feed the littlest lambs or to cut their throats, to tend the sheep or to kill them, to be a Father Kapaun or a Doctor Gosnell. Society is also free to redefine reality, to contracept life, to redefine marriage in terms of civil rights rather than natural law, and to justify the killing of the innocent as a "personal choice." Choices have consequences, and bad choices have bad consequences. When the equivalent of the media in Old Jerusalem, "the council and all the senate of Israel," ordered Peter and the apostles to be silent, they replied, "We must obey God rather than men" (Acts 5:29).

April 21, 2013

No Small Details

Elderly people often wrongly suppose that their recollections are unimportant in the grand scheme of things. And yet their hearers appreciate how apparently random details can evoke the greatest events most movingly. With the *Titanic* anniversary still vivid, there are eyewitness accounts of three priests giving general absolution: Juozas Montvila of Lithuania, Josef Benedikt Peruschitz of Germany, and Thomas Byles of England. Sister Mary Patricia, a religious Sister of Mercy, remembered a woman using her hat to stuff a hole in their lifeboat, and Eva Hart said the orchestra really did play "Nearer My God to Thee." I visited Guglielmo Marconi's widow, who mentioned that her husband had canceled his trip at the last moment and was pleased that his radio system on the *Carpathia* helped to save lives, although other ships closer by had shut down their receivers for the evening. Our own Murray Hill resident J. P. Morgan had a ticket but did not use it.

As "God is in the details," we are grateful for little asides in the Gospel, which the Holy Spirit did not think minor or incidental. Luke's attention to detail made him the patron saint of artists. John usually gave the larger picture with soaring theology, but he does give poignant details in the Resurrection narrative: how he outran Peter; the shroud and napkin neatly folded in the tomb; what the Risen Christ ate in the Upper Room; the wound in Christ's side big enough for a hand to fit in; and the number of fish caught when Christ appeared on the Galilean shore. Our Lord wants us to pay attention to these things: "He that is faithful in that which is least, is faithful also in that which is greater:

and he that is unjust in that which is little, is unjust also in that which is greater" (Luke 16:10).

There is a tradition that the youngest apostle, as an old man, kept saying over and over again, "Little children, love one another," and some of his hearers thought he might be afflicted with the repetitiousness of a mind growing vague with age. He insisted: "I shall keep saying this, for it is what I heard from the lips of the Master." John ended his Gospel account: "There are also many other things that Jesus did, but if these were to be described individually, I do not think the whole world would contain the books that would be written" (John 21:25).

It is old wisdom that the stone on the Easter tomb was rolled away, not so that Jesus might come out, but so that the disciples might go in. With His risen body's character of subtlety, the Lord was no longer limited by His own laws of physics, but He did want us to enter in and see how empty the tomb was, so that we might "know the love of Christ that surpasses knowledge, that you may be filled with all the fullness of God" (Eph. 3:19).

April 22, 2012

ACTING CATHOLIC

The Resurrection of Jesus was not just a spectacle. The first witnesses were both frightened and joyful, but then He poured the Holy Spirit on them, changing them too. The apostles received power to forgive sins, and the lives of all the first Christians were radically changed. Everything glorious in Christian history is the direct result of the Resurrection. The power of the Resurrection gives us saints, and we have more of them now than ever. Cardinal Ratzinger has recently said that moral behavior must be rooted in revelation to be understood and lived fully. While reason discerns the logic of nature and right behavior (pundits condescendingly call this "traditional morality" as if it were an option), the way we ought to behave is completely understood by understanding who God is and who we are in relation to Him. So the Resurrection informs and directs the way we construct society and how political leaders ought to behave. To separate religious beliefs from political reality is morally schizophrenic. The archbishop of Denver wrote about this in Easter week. Archbishop Chaput remarks on the duplicity or, more kindly, ignorance of politicians who claim to be Catholic and take Communion with the Risen Lord while arguing for anti-life legislation. He cites a papal document of 2003, "On Some Questions Regarding the Participation of Catholics in Public Life." Private faith, to be authentic, must have public consequences. Christians "must recognize the legitimacy of differing points of view about the organization of worldly affairs" but they are also "called to reject, as injurious to democratic life, a conception of pluralism that reflects moral relativism." Catholic politicians have a "grave and clear obligation to oppose" any law that attacks innocent human life.

There are many issues implicated in this equation, and they involve medical/moral issues, tax structures, immigration laws, punishment of criminals, housing for the poor, and other issues. But none of these is equal in gravity to the basic right of the unborn to be born. Blessed Pope John XXIII listed this as the first human right. Archbishop Chaput says we should not be fooled: Candidates who claim to be Catholic but who publicly defy Catholic teaching on the sacred principle of life are dishonest public witnesses. "They may try to look Catholic and sound Catholic, but unless they act Catholic in their public service and political choices, they're really a very different kind of creature. And real Catholics should vote accordingly."[38]

Real Catholics could change the world by a personal response to the Resurrection that (1) sends them to the confessional and (2) sends them to the voting booth. The two go together. I am edified each day by the sincere confessions I hear. As your pastor I pray that the way you vote will be a worthy offering at the altar of God and not material for confession.

April 25, 2004

---

[38] Most Rev. Charles J. Chaput, O.F.M. Cap., "How to Tell a Duck from a Fox," *Denver Catholic Register*, April 14, 2004.

A SPIRITUAL ENGINE

Living in New York City means that you have to expect surprises, and the only really surprising surprise would be a day without something unexpected happening. One of the nicest surprises for me recently was a birthday party given me by our children, parents, and teachers. I was invited to the regular CCD session for what I was told would be "Questions and Answers"—but very soon everyone stood up and sang "Happy Birthday." I have a birthday each year, like most people, although I know some grown-ups who claim not to have them, and I also know some children who like birthdays so much that they mark half-year birthdays. It is my lot to have a birthday usually in the lengthening days of Lent, which is not the best party time, although two years ago it was on Easter Day, which is the best feast of all. So it was nice that we could have a birthday party somewhat belated, because each day of the Easter season is a celebration.

Our children also made this a thanksgiving for the Year of Priests. I thank everyone for the huge cake and the flowers, but I cannot possibly express thanks well enough to our young people for the cards and especially their spiritual bouquets. The cards are now nicely bound, and I shall keep them with their fine art, some done with crayons and pencil and others ingeniously cut and pasted. Best of all, though, is the book with promised prayers along with quotations from the Bible, saints, and popes. There are so many Our Fathers, Hail Marys, Glorias, Creeds, visits to the Blessed Sacrament, novenas, and Holy Hours that it would be hard to count them all. I know that these will be a kind of spiritual engine to help our church run better each day. I am especially grateful to have the photographs of our children as a reminder of what a fine church family we have.

There are many challenges to rearing families in our culture, especially in a city, and it is the most heroic kind of vocation, but also the most rewarding. Parents and guardians are specially blessed by God, and children are specially blessed to have such good helpers showing them Our Lord's love. Only a few years ago, our children were a small group, and each year more and more arrive, and we have almost outgrown our space. I often think of the part of James Hilton's novel *Good-bye, Mr. Chips*, where the headmaster pictures passing by in his mind all "his" children he taught over the years—"thousands of them, thousands." I pray that there will be many more. And I also repeat what I said at our party: that I have never worked a day in my life, because when you are very happy with what you are doing, every day is more like a holiday than work.

April 25, 2010

THE NAME

St. John was the only apostle to remain with the Blessed Mother at the Crucifixion, and seared into his mind was the name of Jesus at the top of the Cross. The apostle was always reluctant to mention his own name. In his humility, all that mattered was that he was loved by the Lord. When we receive our names in baptism, they radiate the Holy Name, for every Christian is a spark of the Savior. We should say the Holy Name with reverence, and make reparation when we hear thoughtless people use it as a curse. They do not know its power, but Satan does, and that is why he wants us to twist it if he cannot blot it out.

In the fifteenth century, St. Bernardine of Siena went from town to town preaching, holding a banner emblazoned with the letters IHS, which are the first Greek letters of "Jesus." It was most effective in getting people's attention, and Bernardine now is the patron saint of advertisers. In response to humbugs who accused the saint of making the monogram a kind of magical device, Pope Martin V told him to put a small cross over the letters, to make clear that this was the name of the Crucified One.

Young John survived all the other apostles and, grown old and still remembering how the Master had called them *teknia*, "little children," the night before the Crucifixion, he used the same word: "Little children, I write to you because your sins are forgiven for his name's sake" (1 John 2:12). After Pentecost, with John standing next to him, Peter healed a crippled man by invoking the name of Jesus, which was better than "silver and gold" of which he had none. John and Peter were put on trial for this, and Peter boldly declared, "There is no other name under heaven given among men, whereby we must be saved" (Acts 4:12).

In the spiritual combat of our generation, Satan would tempt timorous Christians to esteem other names as greater than Jesus. Recently a Catholic university covered the letters IHS at the request of politicians, so that the Holy Name would not be seen by the cameras at a public event. When the powers that be were finished, and the letters uncovered again, so also was the weakness of the university exposed. "But whosoever shall deny me before men, him will I also deny before my Father who is in Heaven" (Matt. 10:33).

> St. Peter had no money, but he had the name of Jesus.
> Any institution ashamed of that name will find that its
> golden endowment is tarnished and its silver adds up to
> just thirty pieces.

> Ashamed of Jesus! That dear Friend
> On whom my hopes of Heaven depend!
> No; when I blush, be this my shame
> That I no more revere His Name.[39]

April 26, 2009

---

[39] Joseph Grigg, "Jesus! And Shall It Ever Be," 1765; alt. Benjamin Francis, 1787.

WOLVES AND THE SHEPHERD

The restoration of Grand Central Terminal took several laborious years. It was saved from demolition in reaction to the barbaric destruction of the grand Pennsylvania Station, an aesthetic tragedy paralleling the vandalism by liturgical renovators around the same time. The new and unloved Penn Station insults the aesthetic culture just as do many churches built in that period.

The ceiling of Grand Central retains a small, untouched patch to show the contrast with what it looked like before the cleaning. So too, we need a historical sense to appreciate the contrast between civilization before and after Christ changed the world. He contrasts the world redeemed and unredeemed in His imagery of the Good Shepherd who "lays down his life for his sheep" versus the wolf that "attacks and scatters the sheep" (John 10:11, 12). The contrast is vivid again today, in the saints who follow the Good Shepherd and the evil people who terrorize humanity as wolves.

Often, the wolves do not look like wolves at all. It is easy to spot a terrorist, but most moral degenerates can disguise themselves well. Some wolves are sociopaths with such characteristics as superficial charm, few close friends, unsettling obliviousness to danger, lack of empathy with suffering people while claiming to feel their pain, chronic lying, manipulation by habitual laughter and feigned cheerfulness, and a restless ego. Although they have no "concern for the sheep," their antisocial skills paradoxically help them attain high places in society, supported by the very sheep they would devour. In contrast, the Good Shepherd "is one who lays down his life for his sheep" (John 10:13, 15).

Wolves can fool the sheep, scattering and dividing them through flattery (Ps. 5:10; 78:36; Prov. 28:23; 29:5). It is significant that the same apostle who justly boasted that he flattered no man (1 Thess. 2:5) warned against wolves who disguise themselves in sheep's clothing by perverting the truth (Acts 20:28–31).

Putting aside the tendency to nostalgia, there certainly is enough evidence to warrant a fear that our culture is being seduced by wolfish leaders into a new barbarism as the end of a cycle of civilization. The innovative philosopher of history, Giambattista Vico, described the pattern: "Men first feel necessity, then look for utility, next attend to comfort, still later amuse themselves with pleasure, thence grow dissolute in luxury, and finally go mad and waste their substance."[40]

The new barbarism would be worse than the old, in the words of Churchill in 1940: "a new Dark Age, made more sinister, and perhaps more protracted, by the lights of perverted science." He also warned that the worst enablers of social vandalism are not wolves in sheep's clothing, but sheep in sheep's clothing. Ignorant of the difference between sin and virtue, they naïvely "waste their substance" and welcome wolves while deaf to the voice of the Good Shepherd.

April 26, 2015

---

[40] Giambattista Vico, *Scienza Nuova* (*The New Science*), 1725.

THE SOUL AT EASE

King Charles II said that a gentleman is one who puts those around him at ease. Even on his deathbed he apologized to the courtiers in attendance: "I am sorry, gentlemen, for being such a time a-dying."

When William Penn, as a Quaker, would not doff his hat to the king, the king removed his own.

Puzzled, Penn asked the monarch, "Friend Charles, why dost thou remove *thy* hat?"

The king answered, "Friend William, in circumstances such as these, it is customary for only one man to keep his hat on."

One would risk glibness if not irreverence to say that Christ was a gentleman, but in His human nature He habitually put those around Him at ease. With protocols from the Heavenly Court, He went to lengths in calming people and caring for their comfort. Never did the Lord "lord over" anyone, and if the occasional hypocrite or unjust judge or weak disciple became nervous in His presence, it was the fault of their guilt, for He never deliberately intimidated or shamed anyone.

Once, when a reporter shouted to the thirty-third president: "Give 'em Hell, Harry!" Truman replied, "I don't give them Hell. I just tell the truth about them and they think it's Hell." Our Lord gave people Heaven itself, and if that frightened them it was because their duplicity made Heaven hellish.

In the Resurrection, Our Lord kept putting people at ease, saying: "Peace"; "Do not be afraid"; "Why are you troubled?" He went so far as to let the apostles touch His wounds, and He ate a piece of baked fish to domesticate their incredulity. I expect that the only one He did not have to tell to calm down was His Mother, who was full of grace.

Jesus had no need to apologize for having taken so long to die, because His very agony was a grace. He did another gracious thing by spending the forty days before His Ascension explaining how all the tangled events of history shaped a picture and how the prophets were prophetic. You can tell how well He taught by the way the apostles later wrote their letters, always with that gentle zeal for souls that makes the term "gentleman" inadequate to describe souls so sympathetic.

When Our Lord had "opened their minds to understand the scriptures," He told those in the Upper Room to "stay in the city until you are clothed with power from on high" (Luke 24:45, 49). We know that Peter listened very carefully, for when he was clothed in that elegant spiritual haberdashery that is sanctifying grace, he delicately told the crowd in Jerusalem that they had acted out of ignorance, but if they repented, the Lord would grant them "times of refreshment" (Acts 3:19). For the Lord—unbending to evil and fierce in the face of the Evil One—is also gentle in all His ways.

April 29, 2012

Total Change — and Its Efficient Cause

In 1969, there were those who called the moon landing the "greatest event in history." From various perspectives, there are many contenders for the title. From the combined perspective of everything scientific, moral, and cultural, the Resurrection of Christ was the most important. Everything AD is different from everything BC, in spite of nervous current attempts to eliminate the distinction between eras.

Given the historical ignorance and immaturity of many students today, who demand psychological counseling when they hear public speakers advocating thoughts contrary to their own and who, like Gnostics, even propose that sexes can change by a simple declaration, they will not appreciate the difference the Resurrection made in civilization. The political culture of our day is distressed by candidates who were not taken seriously as they cavorted on the campuses in the 1960s. It is a chilling thought that the spoiled youth on campuses today, rather like what Shakespeare's Brabantio called "The wealthy curled darlings of our nation,"[41] may be our nation's leaders not long from now.

Examine Roman culture before the Resurrection. The noblest characters of the Republic have molded some of the best of our own culture. And yet the pervasive tone of those days was melancholy, fear, and superstition. In the funerary ceremonies, actors portrayed the darkness of

---

[41] William Shakespeare, *Othello*, act 1, scene 2, line 68.

the Underworld, and those who could indulge the luxury of philosophy, tended to identify wisdom as wistful longing.

It is a cliché to compare one's own generation with the decline of the Roman Empire, but clichés become clichés usually by the substance of their accuracy. Even the Augustan Age came at the expense of the simple virtues of the remnant republic. Its religion had no moral component. The *noncupatio* was a request made of some god, with the promise to give something in return, or a *solutio*. The pious deal made no moral demand on the client. Power was the practical god, and anyone who could secure it was justified by the securing. The Triumvirate of Octavian, Mark Antony, and Lepidus was achieved by each betraying his closest relatives and friends. All was accomplished through the manipulation of a complex legal system of tribunes, praetors, quaestors, consuls, and aediles. It seemed neat on the exterior, if raucous.

Then appeared people declaring that a man named Jesus had risen from the dead in a backwater of the empire. Not all of them were slaves and downtrodden—some were relatives of the Flavian emperors and rich families such as the Acilii Glabriones. The politicians accused them of *contemptissima inertia,* by which "contemptible laziness" they meant modesty, contempt for celebrity and public honors, reverence for life, disdain for cruelty, the exaltation of the family, and the indissolubility of marriage.

The Resurrection of Jesus was not a myth invented to bolster this radical shift. It was the efficient cause of the change in the empire and the world.

April 24, 2016

Now Has the Son of Man Been Glorified

Like two bookends, Jesus speaks of His "hour": at the beginning of His ministry, at the wedding in Cana (John 2:4), and at the end, when He says that His hour has come "to be glorified" (John 12:23). That hour of glorification is the unveiling of His divinity, since when He became truly human He never abandoned that divine nature. It was glimpsed at His baptism and at the Transfiguration. At the Last Supper, He spoke of His glory as something that was already there and would soon become visible: "Now has the Son of Man been glorified, and in him God has been glorified. If God has been glorified in him, God will in turn glorify him in himself, and will glorify him very soon" (John 13:31–32).

Watching the Ascension, frail human eyes had a hard time processing that glory in the intellect. The description grasps for words to describe what is beyond familiar physical formulas: "He was lifted up, and a cloud took him from their sight" (Acts 1:9).

His departure would make Him more vividly present. It was not like people on the dock waving wistfully to passengers on a departing ship while the band plays "Now is the hour when we must say goodbye." I remember that scene from the days when the great ocean liners pulled out from the piers down the street from our church. Christ is no longer limited by space, so His Church can be everywhere, with Him present on every altar. There is then a paradox of glory: as Christ leaves, He says, "I am with you always, until the end of the age" (Matt. 28:20).

This is the treasure and confidence of the Church in times when the presence of Christ seems obscured by tragic events and vain people. The beloved apostle John described the Ascension to Polycarp, who became bishop of Smyrna in Asia Minor (present-day Turkey), a city whose architecture can be seen today on the Internet reconstructed by computer-aided design. Before Polycarp passed along John's description to Irenaeus, who became bishop in Lugdunum (present-day Lyons in France), he wrote:

> The faith and the tradition of the churches founded in Germany are no different from those founded among the Spanish and the Celts, in the East, in Egypt, in Libya, and elsewhere in the Mediterranean world. Just as God's creature, the sun, is one and the same the world over, so also does the Church's preaching shine everywhere to enlighten all men who want to come to a knowledge of the truth.
>
> Now of those who speak with authority in the churches, no preacher however forceful will utter anything different—for no one is above the Master—nor will a less forceful preacher diminish what has been handed down. Since our faith is everywhere the same, no one who can say more augments it, nor can anyone who says less diminish it.

May 1, 2016

A GREAT PRINCE, A GREATER SAINT

Nuno Alvares Pereira, born in 1360, was a descendant of Charlemagne and, by the marriage of his daughter to a son of the king of Portugal, became ancestor to many shapers of history, including Catherine of Aragon and Mary Tudor. One of his descendants was Catherine of Bragança, who became queen consort of England by her marriage to Charles II and in whose honor our city's borough of Queens was named. She also popularized tea drinking in England. With his friend Henry the Navigator, Nuno began the "Age of Exploration" and took the gospel to Africa. Columbus might never have sailed without the patronage of Nuno's descendant Queen Isabella. The assassination of another descendant, Archduke Ferdinand, triggered World War I and changed the world again.

On April 26, Pope Benedict XVI, having recognized the miraculous cure of a blind woman by Nuno's intercession, declared him a saint, 578 years after his death in the same year that Joan of Arc was burned. St. Nuno consecrated his life to the Blessed Virgin, whom we crown with flowers in the month of May because she was granted to us as our mother by her Son when He was crowned with thorns.

Nuno engraved the name of Mary on the sword he wielded to protect the people of his land. He secured Portuguese independence from the Kingdom of Castile in battles against tremendous odds: Atoleiros, Aljubarrota, and Valverde. Under a banner emblazoned with Our Lady and St. George, he would stop in the middle of the fighting to fall on his knees in prayer, such as when his six thousand troops were being attacked by a force of more than thirty thousand.

Like Wellington and all true soldiers, he knew that "save for a battle lost, nothing is so tragic as a battle won." Called "the Peacemaker," he nursed his wounded enemies and refused the spoils of battle. When his wife died, he distributed his wealth to his comrades in arms and orphans and became a Carmelite monk. When former foes came to see "Fra Nuno of St. Mary" in his monastery, he showed them his armor beneath his religious habit and warned them he was ready to mount his steed again if anyone harmed the innocent. Sir Galahad was of legend; Nuno was the perfect knight in fact. He died on Easter Day as a priest was reading Our Lord's words from the Cross: "Behold your Mother." His epitaph said:

Here lies that famous Nuno, the Constable, founder of the House of Bragança, excellent general, blessed monk, who during his life on earth so ardently desired the Kingdom of Heaven that after his death, he merited the eternal company of the Saints. His worldly honors were countless, but he turned his back on them. He was a great Prince, but he made himself a humble monk. He founded, built, and endowed this church in which his body rests.

May 3, 2009

Ordinary Magnificence

In the days before professional sports became decadent, with players paid the prodigal salaries of tycoons, the average fan did not have to take out a mortgage to take his family to a game. Players had a more temperate sense of themselves as well. When Bobby Thomson hit "the shot heard 'round the world" at the Polo Grounds on October 3, 1951, he acknowledged the applause and then used a ten-cent token to take the subway home.

Simplicity was an instinct rooted in our nation's original culture, as when Thomas Jefferson took the presidential oath of office and returned to his boarding house, where he waited his turn for dinner, and when Harry Truman left the White House and drove himself back to Missouri with no guards and no pension. He did not pretend to be broke, because he *was* broke. He refused directorships on corporations, saying it would be trafficking in the dignity of the presidential office. It cannot be said that Queen Victoria lived in penury, but she did have her own notion of domesticity when she darned socks for the Prince of Wales in Windsor Castle, humming, "Be it ever so humble, there's no place like home." In her youth, she returned from her coronation in the gilded state coach, took off her ermine robes, put on an apron, and gave her dog a bath.

Each Easter season, one reflects on how the ineffable glory of the Resurrection mingled with utter ordinariness. While endowed with supernatural qualities, Christ looked like nothing more than an ordinary man, and he ate fish and a honeycomb to prove that He was not a ghost. Peter, perhaps partly out of stunned shock, reacted by doing what he had done long before the world's greatest event: "I'm going fishing" (John

21:3). And after the Resurrection, Jesus himself did not twirl about in oriental display. He cooked fish back home in Galilee.

All this was because the Master had a plan for His Church and had to prepare His disciples to preach eternal glory to a world that calculates life in moments of time and measures eternity according to the concepts of space. Christ is too holy to appear exotic, and His mysteries are too profound to mystify. He interprets the mysteries of faith through accessible language and in cogent ways. This is the essence of His love, which is merciful and not condescending. In the sixteenth century, Saint Teresa of Avila had mystical transports while washing dishes, and in the seventeenth century Brother Lawrence "practiced the presence of God" while doing the daily inventory of his monastery. If there is any regret at all in Heaven, it may be the realization that in our short span in this temporal world, we did not discern the magnificence of ordinary things and did not perceive our true home in the House of God.

May 3, 2015

HOLINESS, NOT ENTERTAINMENT

A chief attention of our Holy Father Pope Benedict XVI will be the Sacred Liturgy. *Lex orandi, lex credendi*—that is, "The way we pray shows what we believe." The Pope wrote much about the "reform of the reform" of the Liturgy. By this he meant the correction of abuses that have spread as the result of a false understanding of what the Second Vatican Council intended.

Liturgy is at the heart of converting souls. The dismaying decline in worship in many places has ironically been the result of imposed attempts to "make the Mass more meaningful." There still are some who defend radical changes in the Liturgy, in spite of the statistics that glare at them. Thus the old joke: "The difference between a liturgist and a terrorist is that you can negotiate with a terrorist."

Pope Benedict is a splendid, not a sham, liturgist and will call the world's attention to the Church's heritage, which many Catholics have neglected. Young people have often been deprived of a richness of worship that is rightly theirs. If they fall away, it may be the consequence of not having been taught the true mystery of holiness. They do not need to go to church to be entertained. Worship is not entertainment. The astonishing practice in some churches of parishioners applauding each other and their choirs for their "performances" will be eliminated, when true reform comes. It is no longer done here.

In Eastertide, as part of the Year of the Eucharist, our archdiocese had a procession of the Blessed Sacrament the length of Manhattan, attracting over a thousand at some of the churches visited. Many of our younger parishioners participated. It is a sign of vital revival: this custom was largely lost in the guitar-playing 1970s, but the younger people are recovering it, much to the happiness of many of their seniors who were not swept away in what Pope Benedict has called "the cult of banality." This is threatening and confusing to those who in the last generation thought they could replace the sacred tradition of true adoration, but it is the heart of true renewal of Christian fervor.

In a spiritual anointing, our beloved late Pope John Paul II, when he was dying, assigned the future Benedict XVI the work of preaching the Stations of the Cross on Good Friday. The future Pope said amongst many things: "How often do we celebrate only ourselves without even realizing that He is there!"

"He" refers to Jesus Christ crucified and risen, the great missing person of so many new liturgies, which have become "meaningless dances around the golden calf that is ourselves."

Great days are ahead for our Holy Church, which Pope Benedict has said is young and alive. Or as the converted St. Augustine said, "Late have I loved thee, Beauty ever ancient, ever new."

May 8, 2005

Visible and Invisible

The liturgical calendar is filled with events in the earthly life of Christ. The one time in the year when nothing seems to happen, when chronology is a vacuum, is that space between the Crucifixion and the Resurrection. But the Creed does not admit of such an interpretation. When the Lord seemed to have become still, He was "harrowing Hell."

The point is this: His disappearances are as significant as His appearances. If you assemble the post-Resurrection appearances, including those after the Ascension—namely, to Stephen being martyred, to Paul on the Damascus road, and to John on Patmos—there are fifteen particular appearances. But that also means there were that many disappearances. Each time He vanished, He was doing something unseen. We may not know until we enter eternity what all that involved, but at least it explains why He said before the Ascension that He had to leave us in order to be with us, and why He said that He was going to prepare a place for us.

In the detective story "Silver Blaze," Sherlock Holmes told the Scotland Yard detective Inspector Gregory that the "curious incident of the dog in the night-time" was precisely that the dog did not bark. The silence was as revealing as any sound. This is to be remembered when God seems absent from current events, or distant from us in our daily perplexities. He who never lied said that he would be with us until the end of time.

Rather than despair when God seems absent, the solution is to try to figure out why He is hidden. "Seek the Lord and his strength. Seek his face always" (Ps. 105:4). To want Him to be near is already to be near

Him. "Take comfort; you would not be looking for me if you had not already found me."[42]

The saints have understood Solomon's transporting love poem, the Song of Songs, to be more than an allegory of the love of a man for his beloved: it is a parable of Christ's love for His bride, the Church. St. Bernard understood it also as Christ's love for each soul. As Christ came into the world to seek us, so "there he stands behind our wall, gazing through the windows, peering through the lattice" (Song of Sol. 2:9). But there are times when He acts furtively, vanishing from view, intangible, enticing the soul to long for Him: "I looked for him, but did not find him" (Song of Sol. 3:2).

What seems an absence is a dynamic presence, apprehended by faith as "evidence of things unseen" (Heb. 11:1), influencing events and lives with a power not of this world. "Because you have seen me, you have believed; blessed are those who have not seen and yet have believed" (John 20:29).

May 8, 2016

---

[42] Blaise Pascal, *Pensées* 553.

OBVIOUS TRUTH

The last words spoken by Our Lord from the Cross to the human race were about His Mother. Through St. John He entrusted the spiritual welfare of all of us to her protection. The custom of crowning an image of the Blessed Mother in the month of May, which our children did so elegantly last Sunday, honors the promise and obligation imposed on us from the Cross. Mary has won the "crown of righteousness" (2 Tim. 4:8), the "crown of life" (James 1:12; Rev. 2:10), and the "crown of glory" (1 Pet. 5:4) that Christ offers to all His followers.

Pope John Paul II has consecrated his pontificate to Mary (*Totus Tuus*, "All Yours"). He has asked Catholics throughout the world to join him in the Marian month of May for a special prayer intention: "That the family, founded on the marriage of a man and a woman, may be recognized as the basic cell of human society." The need to pray for such an obvious truth indicates how deeply our culture has sunk into the swamps of degeneracy. An entire generation is being reared in a way oblivious to natural law.

Some politicians promote the destruction of the family and the legalization of counterfeit forms of marriage. Either by ignorance or demagoguery, some will try to lump the issues of abortion and marriage with issues of social polity. They will say we shouldn't be "selective" in giving preeminence to the right to life and authentic marriage over other matters, such as ecology, the death penalty, welfare reform, health care, and so on. Usually, they prefer to remain anonymous and shrink from debate.

Such illogic would never have persuaded a more civilized age. It is a transparent way that the Prince of Lies would confuse people. Policies on air pollution, tax structures, seal hunting, and psoriasis do not have the moral weight of natural law as it pertains to the right to life of the unborn and the integrity of the family. Abortion is intrinsically evil—*malum in se*—and it is not a prudential matter like capital punishment or other issues. Excommunication from God's sacraments is automatic (*latae sententiae*) when one participates in an intrinsic evil.

In the recent march on Washington by pro-abortionists, acts of sacrilege were committed, images of Christ were mocked, and priests and devout Catholics on the sidelines were subjected to obscenities, which the popular media did not report. It was a veritable *Walpurgisnacht*, and this is to be expected since we are engaged in a deep spiritual warfare. In such ugly moments, horrendously encouraged by many public figures who solicit the votes of Catholics, we are invigorated by the beautiful contrast of our Risen Lord and Our Lady, to whom He says, "Arise my Love, my fair one and come away, for the winter is over and done" (Song of Sol. 2:10–11).

May 9, 2004

"It Is the Lord!"

On April 30, Monsignor William F. Guido died peacefully, and his soul was committed to Christ the High Priest. He was the third pastor of the Church of Our Saviour, having previously been an associate pastor at the Church of Our Lady of Victory in the financial district. By coincidence, I succeeded him in that parish, never thinking that someday I would succeed him as pastor here. By another coincidence, our new archbishop, having offered Mass here on May 1 for the Sisters of Life, also offered Monsignor Guido's funeral Mass the next morning. You know my strong view that the word "coincidence" is vague shorthand for Providence. God works all things according to His design and, to the degree that we cooperate with His plans, He makes all things well with us.

As we pray for Monsignor Guido's soul, we also give thanks for all his efforts in his years here to maintain and prosper this parish when it was burdened with heavy debts. We also give thanks that exactly one week after Monsignor Guido's burial, Vincent Druding of this parish was called to the Sacred Priesthood. Monsignor Guido was born in 1918. Vincent Druding was born sixty years later. I was born halfway between the two. So the priestly line goes on from the Resurrection — when Our Savior breathed on the Apostles in the Upper Room, giving them authority to forgive sins.

Whatever age a man is chronologically, when the priestly stole is placed on his shoulders he becomes two thousand as he is united to the office of Christ the Priest. And however old a priest is chronologically when he dies, he is as young as the youthful apostle John, who recognized the voice from the shore and said, "It is the Lord!" That is what every priest says each day when he raises the Blessed Sacrament at the altar.

On this Fifth Sunday of Easter, having been ordained in the Cathedral of Saint Patrick the previous day, Vincent offers Mass for the first time on his own, having concelebrated yesterday with the archbishop. To the Eucharistic thanksgiving, we offer our own prayers of thanksgiving for our first parishioner to be ordained a priest for the archdiocese, and for all the young men of our parish now heeding the call of Christ to do the same.

Christ asked his first apostles, "Have you caught anything?" When they cast their nets into the deep (*duc in altum*), their catch was great. So we pray it will be for Vincent, whom we now call Father Druding, and for all the priests who obey God's command. A nineteenth-century hymn recalls what began many centuries ago:

> God of the prophets! Bless the prophets' sons,
> Elijah's mantle o'er Elisha cast;
> Each age its solemn task may claim but once;
> Make each one nobler, stronger, than the last.

May 10, 2009

GOOD MEMORIES

History is filled with surprising anomalies that catch us up in contradictions. Sir Walter Scott wrote in his poem *Marmion* about the Battle of Flodden Field: "Oh, what a tangled web we weave / when first we practice to deceive!" The battle took place in 1513 while Henry VIII was in France fighting as a member of the Catholic League. His queen, Catherine, eventually to be divorced by him, organized the battle with success.

Meanwhile, Pope Julius II styled Henry "the Most Christian King of France," and although Henry would prove a disappointment in church matters, in 1521 the next Pope, Leo X, declared him "Defender of the Faith," a title Henry kept even after it was rescinded in 1538.

In another anomaly, at the time of the Battle of the Boyne in Ireland in 1690, Pope Alexander VIII supported the House of Orange against the Catholic Stuarts, and ordered that church bells in Rome be rung to celebrate the Protestant victory.

The web of contradiction becomes more entangled in our day when politics are complicated by moral inconsistencies. I cite three examples. First, the birth of Princess Charlotte Elizabeth Diana occasioned celebrations, as the birth of any baby should. During the royal pregnancy, no one had referred to the unborn princess as anything other than a baby. Journalistic attention was focused on whether the infant was a boy or a girl, and what name would be given. Yet by the laws of the realm, the princess was at that time a potentially disposable fetus. No one raised the question of the civil consequences should the unspeakable be done, and the child aborted if judged unsuitable for the line of succession.

Recently, there was rioting in Baltimore—and demonstrations in the streets of many cities—over the death of a young man in police custody. Though that case has yet to be decided in a court of law, it absorbed national attention while at the same time the public slaughter of hundreds of Christians by ISIS received scant commentary. Although no one still calls these ISIS murderers "Junior Varsity,"[43] there persists an ideological aversion to admitting that they are engaged in a most heinous kind of religious persecution.

Lastly, when two Muslim men in Texas, enraged to learn there was a public exhibition of paintings of Mohammed, started shooting at the viewers of the art with machine guns before being shot themselves by law enforcement, editorialists were indignant—at the art. Yet not long before, some of the same editors defended as "legitimate expressions of free speech" a touring exhibition of a picture of the Crucified Christ submerged in urine by Andres Serrano and an image in the Brooklyn Museum that portrayed the Virgin Mary covered with obscenities and elephant dung by Chris Ofili (who was awarded the Turner Prize for his body of work).

Such commentators were negligent of their own inconsistencies. Among the things they forgot, in their moral incoherence, was the advice of Pope Alexander VIII's great-nephew Pietro Cardinal Ottoboni: "Liars need good memories."

May 10, 2015

[43] See "Obama Likens ISIS to 'J.V. Team,'" *New York Times*, January 27, 2014, https://www.nytimes.com/.

CROWNING GLORY

All liturgical celebrations reflect the glory of the Resurrection. Great feasts in May, especially the Ascension, are commentaries on Christ's victory. May is a special time for honoring the Mother of our Risen Lord. The custom developed over a long period.

King Alphonsus X of Castille supplied music for the "Lady Month" of May, and the devotion spread, so that within a few centuries May was identified with Mary—just as June came to be identified with the Heart of Jesus and October with the Rosary.

The last word Our Lord spoke to the human race from the Cross was "Mother." Mary shows the way to her Son. People who try to find God without His Mother will get lost, and those who call themselves Christian without calling on Mary are confused children. All honor paid to Mary is tribute to her Risen Son. Had Christ not risen from the grave, the most famous woman in history would be unknown, as if she had never existed.

The fair month of May belongs to the "Mother of Fair Love." The first day of May was an ancient celebration of the start of plant growth. Hard and cynical people replaced the maypole with coarse Communist parades, but that illusion of a worker's paradise without God has fallen on the ash heap of history. Ancient Romans dedicated May to the goddess of blossoms, Flora, and prepared for her feast with late April "floral games" (*ludi florales*). Christianity did not extrapolate a Marian month from these customs; these customs were an unconscious intuition that there would someday be a Blessed Mother.

The bishops of the United States in 1987 approved this direction: "Coronation is one form of reverence frequently shown to images of the

Blessed Virgin Mary.... It is especially from the end of the 16th century that in the West the practice became widespread.... The popes not only endorsed this devout custom but 'on many occasions, either personally or through bishop-delegates, carried out the coronation of Marian images.'" Mary is ceremoniously crowned with flowers and jewels because she is the mother of the messianic King and his perfect follower.

Saints such as Elizabeth Ann Seton, Frances Cabrini, and Teresa of Calcutta (to be beatified October 19) are instinctively called "Mother" because of their maternal grace. Great as the title "saint" is, every man and woman harbors in the heart a hushed reverence for the title "mother." This Sunday the parish crowns Holy Mary, commending our earthly mothers, living and deceased, to the care of Our Lord—who gave us His own Mother in the midst of His deepest suffering for the whole world.

May 11, 2003

PROTECTION FROM ERROR

The singular and mysterious events surrounding the apparitions at Fatima in 1917, which will be celebrated on May 13, were deemed by the Church to be, while not essential doctrine, since all revelation ended with the death of the last apostle, certainly "worthy of belief." In 2010, Pope Benedict XVI said that they have a "permanent and ongoing significance" which "could even be extended to include the suffering the Church is going through today." Last year on October 13—the anniversary of the "Miracle of the Sun"—Pope Francis consecrated the world to Mary, standing before a statue of Our Lady of Fatima.

The Church suffers in many ways, most conspicuously (even if neglected by much of the secular media) by physical persecution in many countries. Indeed, this oppression is on the increase. On May 2, the Holy Father said, in an apparent reference to Syria, "I cried when I saw reports on the news of Christians crucified in a certain country that is not Christian."

A subtler form of suffering is by heresy. The word means choosing a wrong understanding of the truth, and this can be more dangerous than physical wounds, as it damages souls and not just bodies. Martyrdom glorifies and enriches the Church, while the spread of error weakens the Body of Christ on earth.

While frequently lauding the inestimable gift of women religious to the Church through their work of prayer, education, and manifold charities (one quarter of all the world's humanitarian institutions are sponsored by the Catholic Church, many of them through women religious), Pope Francis has called attention to heresy among some communities of consecrated religious. His Prefect for the Congregation of the Doctrine of the Faith, Cardinal Gerhard Müller, said in an official letter on April 30 that they have succumbed "to fundamental errors regarding the omnipotence of God, the Incarnation of Christ, the reality of Original Sin, the necessity of salvation and the definitive nature of the salvific action of Christ in the Paschal Mystery."[44] The Prefect expressed concern that the Leadership Conference of Women Religious in particular has endorsed certain kinds of teaching that offer "a vision of God, the cosmos, and the human person divergent from or opposed to Revelation [and that endorsement of such a vision] evidences that a *de facto* movement beyond the Church and sound Christian faith has already occurred."[45]

Demographically, misguided communities are fading away in their embrace of ephemeral heresies, while many new orders are growing by the strength of "powers of discernment trained by constant practice to distinguish good from evil" (Heb. 5:14). These declines caused by error and the simultaneous growth nurtured by truth and orthodoxy have a parallel in the life of local churches, too. "Where there is no vision, the people perish: but he that keeps the law, happy is he" (Prov. 29:18).

As May is the month of Mary by virtue of its loveliness, it is prime time to ask her intercession for the whole Church, our archdiocese, our parishes, and ourselves.

May 11, 2014

---

[44] Cardinal Gerhard Müller, Opening remarks at the meeting of the superiors of the Congregation for the Doctrine of the Faith with the presidency of the Leadership Conference of Women Religious, April 30, 2014.

[45] Ibid.

THE LIGHTS OF DIVINITY

Manhattan has never seen so many buildings rising at the same time. Cranes tower at dizzying heights. Most new structures are sterile glass boxes, but there are a few eccentric structures designed by celebrity architects, or "starchitects," as they are called, and those aspiring to distinction. They deliberately look as if they are about to fall. These may attract attention, like the Leaning Tower of Pisa, but that tower was not originally designed to lean.

Drawing on classical norms, St. Thomas Aquinas proposed that the attributes that make a thing beautiful are integrity, proportion, and clarity. Integrity is the suitability for its function. Proportion is the symmetry by which its parts fit and work together. Clarity is the radiance that gives delight to the eye and is chiefly the ineffable quality that gives delight to the beholder. Not to dramatize or condemn, it is nonetheless the case that an architect who contradicts those norms is mocking the order of creation itself.

Our Lord sent the Holy Spirit to lead His Church into all truth. The Third Person of the Holy Trinity, who is the bond of love between the Father and the Son, unites the Christian (by "adoption" through baptism) with God's beauty. Christ is the Way (integrity) and the Truth (proportion) and the Life (clarity). His purpose is to show us the Father; His truth is that He and the Father are one, and His clarity is the light of His divinity. Put those three together, and you have perfection.

Our culture is rather like that of Ephesus when St. Paul went there. Most people know nothing of what Christ has accomplished, and even some who think they are Christians could say, "We have never even heard that there is a Holy Spirit" (Acts 19:2). Our Lord tasked His followers—and we are the newest of them—to bring others to the beauty of truth. St. John Paul II said that his favorite line in the Bible was "The truth shall make you free" (John 8:32). It must also be the most hated line of the Prince of Lies. When he lies, he persuades people that his deceits are beautiful. He can even appear in attractive form himself. But his enticements are nothing but glitz, and in his lack of integrity, proportion, and clarity, cooperation with him through sinning makes his minions ugly. God's grace is the opposite. In the words of a hymn written by Samuel Crossman in 1664: "Love to the loveless shown, that they might lovely be."

The most beautiful of God's creatures are the saints, who let the Holy Spirit dwell in them. "Your beauty should not come from outward adornment such as braided hair or gold jewelry or fine clothes, but from the inner disposition of your heart, the unfading beauty of a gentle and quiet spirit, which is precious in God's sight" (1 Pet. 3:3–4).

May 15, 2016

CIVILITY AND EVIL

The ordination of new priests for our archdiocese last week was accompanied by delightful receptions well suited for the month of May. Graceful conviviality is becoming as rare in our coarsened culture as when the pagan Romans were astonished by the celebratory *refrigeria*[46] of the Christians, free of the vulgarity and cruelty that the post-republican empire had come to equate with fun.

Loss of reverence for innocent life corrupts the manners that were the signature of the classical ages and whose exchange for gaudy excess was the emblem of their decadence. The way people dress and speak and treat one another signals their self-perception. When civility is disdained as bourgeois, the servant is deprived of his royal dignity as a child of God, and the king is absolved of his duty to revere those he governs.

Cardinal Newman defined the gentleman, and by inference the lady, in cadences that have become almost as incomprehensible as the terms "gentleman" and "lady" themselves. "It is almost a definition of a gentleman to say he is one who never inflicts pain." He speaks of moral care for the consciences of others. The gentleman puts others at ease and "makes light of favors while he does them, and seems to be receiving when he is conferring." He does not slander or gossip, treats his enemy as a potential friend and is "merciful to the absurd."

---

[46] Among the early Christians in Rome, a *refrigerium* (refreshment) was a meal taken in a graveyard or catacomb to pray for a departed soul—on the ninth day after burial, and annually thereafter.

This is not the low discourse of modern politics and journalism. So annually we now have the perfect storm of barbarism at the White House Correspondents Dinner. Each year it gets worse, and this year a woman—hired as a comedienne—failed in the useful role of court jester, wishing on those "traitors" she did not like sickness and worse. The highest officials of our land joined in the harsh laughter and added sexual innuendoes. Like the Vandals who ridiculed the noble Roman senators, they mocked abstinence from vice and dissected virtue as weakness. Their cynicism matched Oscar Wilde's when he said that a gentleman is one who never inflicts pain unintentionally.

Drawing on the fifth century *Psychomachia* of Prudentius, medieval writers charted kindness among the "heavenly virtues" to cure envy, which is a motive for cruelty, and pride, which is the alchemy of disdain. Newman knew, like St. Paul, that classical kindness is only aesthetical moral furniture without the love of the Holy Spirit (see 2 Cor. 6:6). But he also knew that uncourtly behavior courts blaspheming the Holy Spirit. When journalists approve the rants of poor breeding as "just comedy" and its victims as "fair game," they approve the sadism of Petronius and the vulgarity of Rabelais. They shift from Mark Twain, who could disagree without being disagreeable, to Fellini, who relished degradation. For all his populism, Dickens was a rank snob when he said the term "American gentleman" was a self-contradiction. We should not want to prove him right.

May 17, 2009

HEAVEN'S FIRST LAW

I am tempted to detect more than merely accidental circumstance in the fact that the apostles chose seven men as the first deacons: "Stephen, a man full of faith and of the Holy Spirit, together with Philip, Prochorus, Nicanor, Timon, Parmenas, and Nicolaus of Antioch, a convert to Judaism" (Acts 6:5). There is an elegant symmetry in the seven days of creation and consequent replications of that number in the weekly Sabbath cycle and so forth, and it seems to reach full bloom in the Incarnation, with the seven sacraments and the seven last words from the Cross.

Our Incarnate Lord describes Himself with seven images: I am the Light of the World (John 8:12; 9:5); I am the Way and the Truth and the Life (John 14:6); I am the Bread of Heaven (see John 6:41); I am the Good Shepherd (John 10:11, 14); I am the Gate of the Sheepfold (John 10:9); I am the Resurrection (John 11:25); and I am the Vine (John 15:5). There is an order in the Church reflected in the order of the universe. The Catholic poet Alexander Pope said, "Order is heaven's first law." God does nothing by chance, and His every action is part of a pattern. Just as defects in the natural order are understood as defects only because the source of all things is perfect, so are defects in the moral order affronts to perceived human dignity. These defects are commonly called sins, but the original sin, called pride, is the prehistoric rebellion against the fact of order itself.

The seven images that Christ uses to explain Himself in terms coherent to our limited intelligence make sense only when we realize that each of them is attached to and depends upon the I AM. That is the identity of God, the source of all being and order.

Our culture is going through an identity crisis in virtually every aspect of its existence: politically, economically, morally, and intellectually. There is even disarray in how to identify biological and psychological realities. Instead of male and female, some would propose an alphabet soup of gender confusion, with new letters waiting to be added in the maelstrom of disorder.

God's creatures self-destruct when they separate themselves from the I AM, and instead of praising their Creator, there is left only a whimpering question: What AM I?

Confusion about the self can be resolved by listening to Our Lord as He speaks in the Gospel passage appointed for this Sunday (John 14:1–12). An instinctive grace shines in the way He uses "I am" seven times: I am going to prepare a place for you; where I am you may be too; the place where I am going; I am the Way and the Truth and the Life; I am in the Father and the Father is in me; you must believe me when I say that I am; I am going to the Father.

May 18, 2014

THE HOLY SPIRIT

When St. Paul came across some people in the Turkish town of Ephesus who believed in Jesus, they told him, "We have never even heard that there is a Holy Spirit." So Paul baptized and confirmed them (Acts 19:2, 5). In the sacrament of confirmation, the Holy Spirit completes His work begun in baptism, which washes away original sin, by placing ("infusing" or "sealing") seven gifts in the soul. These help one live the Christian life by perfecting the virtues.

God does everything for a purpose. Four of the gifts of the Holy Spirit perfect the intellectual virtues. The purpose of the gift of *understanding* is to give an intuitive and penetrating perception of truth. *Wisdom* perfects love, by enabling a right appreciation of how God's love works. *Knowledge*, by discerning the divine plan in events, perfects the virtue of hope. *Counsel* increases prudence. Those four gifts, then, perfect the virtues pertaining to the intellect. The intellect is one element of the soul. Three other gifts perfect the other part of the soul which is the will. The gift of *piety* perfects the virtue of justice by helping us give to others what is properly theirs, refining our relations with others and most especially with God. *Fortitude* strengthens ordinary courage in the face of dangers. *Fear of the Lord* perfects the virtue of temperance by disciplining unruly desires and destructive appetites. It aims our temper against evil and helps us avoid losing our temper.

One could live a virtuous life without the supernatural gifts of the Holy Spirit. So we have the noble pagans of antiquity and the high-minded humanitarians of our culture. The gifts of the Holy Spirit move the soul from philanthropy to sanctity, transforming the human being into something very like God Himself. There is one God, but He can work through His sons and daughters who make themselves available to His gifts.

A toaster is not much good unless it is plugged in. A car gets nowhere unless the ignition is turned on. The day is not eventful until you get out of bed. These homey metaphors are reminders that we need the Holy Spirit. Many earnest people are like those disciples in Ephesus who believed in Jesus but did not know there was a Holy Spirit. Parishes can lapse back into that ignorance, which is worse than starting out ignorant. Frequent confession and Communion help keep the seven gifts alive. And when they are alive, they can change the whole neighborhood, city, and all of civilization.

One of St. Paul's successors, a bishop, will confirm parishioners this Sunday, and will give Our Lord in the Blessed Sacrament to some of our young ones for the first time. This should enliven the whole parish.

May 19, 2002

PUBLISHED IGNORANCE

Writers know the immeasurable blessing of a good editor who will check facts. Generally speaking, though, editing is not what it used to be. In reporting matters of church and religion, there is a specially glaring neglect of facts. And not knowing much about a subject makes some writers freer in what they will say about it. This certainly contradicts the way of the Holy Spirit, given to the Church on Pentecost, who Our Lord promises will lead us to all truth.

When the Pope was in Brazil, he addressed millions of people. On one of those days, a major news service virtually ignored that while reporting with astonishment that a U.S. primary-election candidate had drawn an audience of three thousand. Reading editorials about the decline of faith at the same time the Pope outdraws any secular figure reminds one of Yogi Berra's comment about a restaurant — that no one goes there anymore because it is too crowded.

The April 2 issue of the *New Yorker* ran a long article entitled "The Pope and Islam," which almost dazzled any informed reader with the number of mistakes that could easily have been avoided by an editor who had read the documents being criticized. The burden of the piece was that Pope Benedict has broken with his predecessor in his analysis of the issues. Pope John Paul II, whom the article wrongly said had been a young theological adviser at the Council (Wojtyla was a bishop then, and Ratzinger was a young adviser, or *peritus*), was said to have been more moderate in his account of the theology and anthropology of Islam. A good fact checker would have pointed out that this turned reality upside down. What Pope Benedict XVI said about faith and reason and enlightened thought in his famous Regensburg lecture was a consistent explanation of what Pope John Paul II wrote in his encyclical *Fides et Ratio*. It is also astonishing that the writer failed to understand the important role that Ratzinger had played as a theological voice in the formulation of his predecessor's teaching.

Hasty writers tend to summon up marginal opinions of theologians who agree with them rather than with the Church. At the same time that some of these sources were quoted disapproving of the Regensburg lecture, a friend of mine who is a Nobel laureate, and not a Catholic, and perhaps even agnostic, told me that he thought that Pope Benedict's comments at Regensburg were brilliant.

George Weigel, the noted commentator on the papacy and frequent visitor to our parish, has said that some of these so-called experts who are stuck in the worldview of the 1960s and are bewildered by present realities, resemble those World War II soldiers who were isolated for a generation on remote Pacific islands unaware that their war had ended and that things are very different now. His advice to them: "It's over. Get over it."

May 20, 2007

You Shall Be My Witnesses

Scourging with whips in the Roman style could kill a man. St. Paul was scourged five times and on occasion presumed dead. He endured this because he had been converted by the Risen Christ. Accustomed to forensic testing, Sir Edward Clark wrote: "As a lawyer I have made a prolonged study of the evidence for the first Easter. To me the evidence is conclusive, and over and over again in the High Court I have secured the verdict on evidence not nearly so compelling. As a lawyer I accept it unreservedly as the testimony of men to facts that they were able to substantiate."

St. Luke was a pioneer historian in a time when historical analysis barely existed. He writes that Jesus "presented Himself alive, after His suffering, by many convincing proofs, appearing to them over a period of forty days, and speaking of the things concerning the kingdom of God" (Acts 1:3).

Mary Magdalene was startled by her encounter with Christ in the garden on Easter morning. She grabbed hold of His feet and then told the disciples, "I have seen the Lord" (John 20:18). Jesus ordered several other women who saw Him to tell the disciples to meet Him in Galilee (Matt. 28:9–10). On the Emmaus road He took two disciples by surprise (Luke 24:12–32) and then appeared to ten of the Apostles in the Upper Room (Luke 24:36–43).

A week later He appeared to the Eleven in the room, although the doors were bolted shut (John 20:26). In deference to human incredulity based on our limited physics, He showed them His wounds. In Galilee a little later, He appeared on the shore of the lake, helped His disciples catch 153 fish, fed them, and then talked privately with Peter for a second time (John 21:1–25; see Luke 24:33–35; 1 Cor. 15:5). He appeared to the Eleven who "saw Him, and worshipped Him" and commissioned them to preach.

Five hundred people saw Him on one occasion, and most of them were still alive to describe it thirty years later (1 Cor. 15:6). St. James saw Him, and then His Ascension into glory was witnessed by the disciples near Bethany (Acts 1:9–12): "He was taken up, and a cloud received Him out of their sight." Later, St. Paul says, "As it were to one untimely born, He appeared to me also" (1 Cor. 15:8).

The greatest evidence of the Resurrection is the Church. This Sunday in our little acre of God's Kingdom young people receive their First Communion and are confirmed with the seven gifts of the Holy Spirit. Jesus planned this: "You shall receive power when the Holy Spirit has come upon you; and you shall be my witnesses in Jerusalem and in all Judaea and Samaria, and to the end of the earth" (Acts 1:8).

May 23, 2004

ALWAYS A GIFT

The Family Life/Respect Life Office of the archdiocese, in cooperation with the bishops of all eight dioceses in the state of New York, alerts Catholics to two radical proposals promoting abortion on demand. These are the "Freedom of Choice Act" (FOCA) in the U.S. Congress and the New York State "Reproductive Health Act" (previously known as RHAPP). Among the facts that the secular media tend not to explain are:

1. FOCA and RHAPP would make a "fundamental right" to abortion equivalent to free speech and the right to vote, and would forbid without exception any interference with that right.

2. FOCA and RHAPP would prohibit parental notification, clinic regulation, bans on partial-birth, and late-term abortions.

3. FOCA and RHAPP would eliminate the federal Hyde Amendment, which restricts federal Medicaid funding of abortions and would force all Americans to subsidize abortion through their tax dollars.

4. FOCA and RHAPP would threaten the freedom of conscience of pro-life doctors and nurses and health-care workers.

5. FOCA and RHAPP would threaten Catholic hospitals, social-service agencies, and schools. The government could deny licenses and funding to hospitals that do not permit abortions and would require schools to make abortion referrals and mandate abortion coverage in all insurance plans.

6. FOCA and RHAPP would jeopardize any programs that encourage pregnant women to bring their babies to term, by ruling them as "discriminatory."

7. RHAPP would allow unqualified medical professionals such as midwives and nurse practitioners to perform abortions.

All who defend the right to life as civilization's fundamental civil right are urged to send messages to their legislators. More information may be had through the archdiocesan web site: www.FLRL.org.

During recent political elections, warnings about such legislation were dismissed as demagoguery and hysteria. As in other hapless times in history, many said, "It couldn't happen here." It is happening, and the slide is being greased by smooth-sounding words and affable promises of "creative change." Rational arguments are drowned out by crowds shouting slogans. In these times the Church asserts her vocation to stand alone against a cruel tide.

In the 1930s Cardinal Faulhaber of Munich risked his life to decry his government's eugenics policies: "I have deemed it my duty to speak out in this ethico-legal, non-political question, for as a Catholic bishop I may not remain silent when the preservation of the moral foundations of all public order is at stake." On June 29, 1951, a year before his death, the cardinal ordained to the priesthood a young man who is now Pope Benedict XVI.

In 2007, that Pope said: "Selfishness and fear are at the root of [pro-abortion] legislation. We in the Church have a great struggle to defend life.... Life is a gift, not a threat. The Church says life is beautiful; it is not something to doubt but it is a gift even when it is lived in difficult circumstances. It is always a gift."[47]

May 24, 2009

---

[47] Philip Pullella, "Pope Warns Catholic Politicians Who Back Abortion," Reuters, May 9, 2007, http://www.reuters.com/.

Yes, Our Bodies Are Sacred

The Gnostic heresy has been smoldering over the centuries like a low-grade fever, never killing Christianity, but debilitating Christian life when it is not detected. Gnosticism is a denial of the divine origin of creation, holding that material reality comes from evil energies and thus is contrary to spiritual good. The Gnostic denies that spiritual goodness could have anything to do with "things." Christian sacramentalism is a scandal to Gnosticism, because it holds that God Himself works through creatures. The feast of Corpus Christi celebrates the sublime mystery in which bread and wine become the actual Body and Blood of Christ. Gnosticism finds this "unspiritual"; even some Christians succumb to this fever and think that the Eucharist is "only a symbol."

Marriage is one of the seven sacraments, dignified by the first miracle performed by Christ at a wedding. Our Lord calls Himself the Bridegroom in a hopeful rejection of Gnostic pessimism about matter. The Gnostic perceives our flesh as a curse and rejects marriage because it exalts the body. This opposes the Christian view of marriage as part of God's plan encoded in nature, with the man loving his wife as Christ loves the Church, in a union open to the procreation of children as the hope of the world. Gnosticism has typically rejected childbearing along with sacred marriage.

The recent 4–3 decision of the California Supreme Court allowing same-sex unions to be defined as marriages was not only a species of judicial overreach, like the U.S. Supreme Court decision legalizing abortion. It was an exercise of Gnostic pessimism that rejected the will of 61 percent of the California electorate and discarded what has been the sense of civilized societies for at least six thousand years. The early Gnostics specifically urged the separation of conjugal union from marriage. In the twentieth century, a similar contempt for natural law promoted artificial contraception, which, while decreasing populations to dangerously low levels, also helped to double the national divorce rate in the space of twenty years. And research by Yale and Catholic universities in the *American Sociological Review* showed that couples who live together before marriage are 80 percent more likely to end up divorced.

The Catholic Bishops Conference of California has said that the decision of California's high court "opens the door for policymakers to deconstruct traditional marriage and create another institution under the guise of equal protection." Simultaneously, the White House stated, "President Bush has always believed marriage is a sacred institution between a man and a woman. It's unfortunate when activist judges continue to seek to redefine marriage by court order—without regard for the will of the people."

On the feast of Corpus Christi, we should also give thanks for Pope Paul VI, who struggled against his own distaste for confrontation to warn boldly that the Gnostic fever would lead to the moral absurdities now threatening civilization.

May 25, 2008

STRATEGIST OF THE SOUL

The feast of St. Philip Neri (1515–1595) falls this Monday, on the same day that the civil calendar memorializes those who gave their lives in the service of our country. Philip was a soldier, too, albeit a soldier of Christ, wearing "the helmet of salvation and the sword of the Spirit, which is the word of God" (Eph. 6:17). He lived in a decadent time when many who called themselves Christians chose to be pacifists in the spiritual combat against the world, the flesh, and the Devil.

In the battle for souls, Philip's most effective weapons were gentleness and mercy, though he was also a master of "tough love" when it was necessary to correct those inclined to be spiritual deserters. Although he was reared in Florence, Philip's pastoral triumphs gained him the title "Apostle of Rome." It was said of the emperor Augustus that he found Rome brick and left it marble, and in a moral sense the same might be said of Philip. The Sacred City was not so sacred in the minds of many, and his chief weapon for reforming it was penance.

After eighteen years in Rome, Philip was ordained at the age of thirty-five. He polished rough souls every day in the confessional, where he might be found at all hours of the day and night for forty-five years. In the words of Blessed John Henry Newman, who joined the saint's Oratory three centuries later, "He was the teacher and director of artisans, mechanics, cashiers in banks, merchants, workers in gold, artists, men of science. He was consulted by monks, canons, lawyers, physicians, courtiers; ladies of the highest rank, convicts going to execution, engaged in their turn his solicitude and prayers."[48] The oratorio is an audible relic of St. Philip: he invented that musical form as a means of catechesis. His magnetic appeal to the most stubborn and cynical types of people seems hardly less miraculous than the way he sometimes levitated during Mass, requiring that he offer the Holy Sacrifice privately. The Pope prudently, if understatedly, explained that the spectacle might distract the faithful.

Refusing high clerical rank and disdaining any sort of human honor, Philip's power intimidated the Prince of Lies as much as any earthly prince. There is a lesson in this for our own urban culture, and certainly for us here—providentially located in Hell's Kitchen. The temptation is for the Church to give up on spiritual combat and retreat to the suburbs. This is a false strategy, since no terrain, concrete or bucolic, offers a complete escape from the Church's field of combat. While consolidation of strength is a necessary strategy, there is no substitute for victory. If General MacArthur maintained that principle with earthly effect, so much more do the saints struggle, knowing that Christ has already won the victory, but also aware that to flee the field is to lose Him forever.

May 25, 2014

---

[48] John Henry Newman, Sermon 12: The Mission of St. Philip, part 2.

JOY AND HOLY FEAR

The one thing God cannot do is contradict Himself. This is proof of His omnipotence, for as Truth, to lie would be to cancel Himself out. Consequently, when there seem to be contradictions in His inspired Scriptures, the task for mankind is to figure out why apparent contradictions are really hidden consistencies.

For instance, God told Abraham: "Do not be afraid" (Gen. 26:24), and when, as Christ, He rose from death, He told the women at the tomb the same thing (Matt. 28:10). How is it, then, that "The fear of the LORD is the beginning of wisdom" (Prov. 9:10)? And why does God say, "My covenant with him was one of life and peace, and I gave them to him. It was a covenant of fear, and he feared me" (Mal. 2:5)? And why is the fear of the Lord one of the "gifts" of the Holy Spirit?

The apparent contradiction is reconciled by God Himself: "And now, Israel, what doth the LORD thy God require of thee, but to fear the LORD thy God, to walk in all his ways, and to love him, and to serve the LORD thy God with all thy heart and with all thy soul" (Deut. 10:12).

That love is born of holy fear, or what we would call "awe," and it is an awe as transportingly joyful as the dark fear—which "perfect love casts out" (1 John 4:18)—is frightful.

Dread, or "servile" fear, in Hebrew is *pachad*. Synonymous with that is *yir'ah*, but that can also mean "holy wonder" or "awe." Jesus Christ, who is the incarnation of the love that uttered all creation into existence, casts out the terror of *pachad* and infuses the soul with the bliss of *yir'ah*.

In the Eucharist, the *Kyrie eleison* (Lord have mercy!) is penitential in tone but only because it is inspired by awe at God's majesty. It is an acclamation and not a gasp of horror. It was with joy that St. Thomas cried out, "My Lord and my God!" at the sight of Christ's wounds (John 20:28).

Like breathing, which we take for granted even though we would die without it, there never is a moment when the Holy Mass is not being prayed somewhere in the world. To take it for granted is to forsake our wondering awe at knowing that Christ grants it. This Sunday, one of our parishioners, John Wilson, will offer his first Mass, having been ordained to the priesthood the day before. But if we are faithful to the Holy Spirit's gift of holy fear, each Mass should be as our first Mass, our last Mass, and our only Mass.

Without holy fear, there would be only dread. Perhaps that explains why our culture is so burdened with "phobias" and so unacquainted with awe at our Eucharistic Lord. "And behold, I am with you always, to the end of the age" (Matt. 28:20).

May 29, 2016

PATIENCE

The child in the backseat asks "Are we there yet?" and the psalmist pleads "*Usquequo, Domine?* (How long, O Lord? [Psalm 13:1]). Patience is a difficult virtue. As we prepare to observe the seventieth anniversary of the Normandy Invasion, we know that only those who were alive then can describe the excruciating months and days of waiting for what President Franklin D. Roosevelt called the "poignant hour."

Our Lord was patient with His apostles: "Have I been with you so long, Philip, and do you still not understand?" (John 14:9). In the days between His Ascension and Pentecost, He enjoined His followers to be patient: "And being assembled together with them, he commanded them not to depart from Jerusalem, but to wait for the Promise of the Father" (Acts 1:4).

Patience is waiting without complaint. After the Resurrection, those who had been great complainers early on no longer murmured, but filled the days with great rejoicing, singing, and praying in anticipation of the unspecified day ("not many days" was all the Master said) when the Holy Spirit would give birth to the Church. That came to pass on the fiftieth day after Our Lord's Resurrection. The Resurrection had coincided with the ancient Jewish feast of the First Fruits (Lev. 23:15–16). Christ had risen on that feast, becoming the fruition of salvation history. The Holy Spirit then came down on Mary and the apostles to fill their hearts on the Jewish feast of Pentecost—which celebrated the giving of the Law on Mount Sinai. Now the letter of that Law would be fulfilled by the Spirit who gives life to the Law.

The Jews calculated the date of Pentecost from the first Sabbath after Passover. Thus, Pentecost followed Christ's Resurrection not fifty but forty-nine days later, and the ten days of waiting following the Ascension were actually nine. In the Levitical system, however, the ninth day marks the conclusion of a feast and the start of a new day lived in consequence of waiting for it. So novenas are nine days of prayers in anticipation of the tenth day.

The "relativity" of natural time is harder to understand than the relativity of moral time. For instance, one hour of pain seems much longer than one hour of pleasure, and the years of waiting for marriage are not as nerve-racking as the few minutes before the wedding. In each instance, the exercise of patience ceases to be a burden, knowing that the anticipated outcome will be realized. St. Peter was an impatient man until the Resurrection. Then he embraced the truth of eternity when he embraced the Risen Lord, and that made all the difference. He came to understand that "with the Lord one day is as a thousand years, and a thousand years are as one day" (2 Pet. 3:8).

So, patience is based on trust, and trust changes endurance into joy: "For the revelation awaits an appointed time; it speaks of the end and will not prove false. Though it linger, wait for it; it will certainly come and will not delay" (Hab. 2:3).

June 1, 2014

Sophia Institute

Sophia Institute is a nonprofit institution that seeks to nurture the spiritual, moral, and cultural life of souls and to spread the Gospel of Christ in conformity with the authentic teachings of the Roman Catholic Church.

Sophia Institute Press fulfills this mission by offering translations, reprints, and new publications that afford readers a rich source of the enduring wisdom of mankind.

Sophia Institute also operates two popular online Catholic resources: CrisisMagazine.com and CatholicExchange.com.

Crisis Magazine provides insightful cultural analysis that arms readers with the arguments necessary for navigating the ideological and theological minefields of the day. *Catholic Exchange* provides world news from a Catholic perspective as well as daily devotionals and articles that will help you to grow in holiness and live a life consistent with the teachings of the Church.

In 2013, Sophia Institute launched Sophia Institute for Teachers to renew and rebuild Catholic culture through service to Catholic education. With the goal of nurturing the spiritual, moral, and cultural life of souls, and an abiding respect for the role and work of teachers, we strive to provide materials and programs that are at once enlightening to the mind and ennobling to the heart; faithful and complete, as well as useful and practical.

Sophia Institute gratefully recognizes the Solidarity Association for preserving and encouraging the growth of our apostolate over the course of many years. Without their generous and timely support, this book would not be in your hands.

www.SophiaInstitute.com
www.CatholicExchange.com
www.CrisisMagazine.com
www.SophiaInstituteforTeachers.org